TABLE OF

Appointment and Qualifications

To become a notary public you must meet all of the following requirements: (Government Code section 8201)

- Be a legal resident of the State of California;
- Be at least 18 years of age;
- Satisfactorily complete a course of study approved by the Secretary of State;
- Pass a written examination prescribed by the Secretary of State; and
- Pass a background check.

To determine if a person meets the requirements to fulfill the responsibilities of the position, a completed application and a 2" x 2" color passport photograph of the applicant shall be submitted at the examination site, then forwarded to the Secretary of State's office and reviewed by Secretary of State staff for qualifying information. (Government Code section 8201.5)

To assist the Secretary of State in determining the identity of an applicant and whether the applicant has been convicted of a disqualifying crime, state law requires all applicants to be fingerprinted as part of a thorough background check prior to being granted an appointment as a notary public. (Government Code section 8201.1) Information concerning the fingerprinting requirements will be mailed to candidates who pass the examination.

Convictions

Applicants are required to disclose on their applications all arrests for which trials are pending and all convictions, including convictions that have been dismissed under Penal Code section 1203.4 or 1203.4a. If you have any questions concerning the disclosure of convictions or arrests, contact the Secretary of State's office prior to signing the application. If you do not recall the specifics about your arrest(s) and/or conviction(s), you can contact the California Department of Justice at (916) 227-3849.

The Secretary of State may deny an application for the following reasons:

- Failure to disclose any conviction;
- Conviction of a felony; or
- Conviction of a disqualifying lesser offense.

The applicant has the right to appeal the denial through the administrative hearing process. (Government Code section 8214.3) For a complete list of reasons the Secretary of State may deny an application, please refer to Government Code section 8214.1. Refer to the Secretary of State's *Notary Public Disciplinary Guidelines* for a list of the most common disqualifying convictions. The disciplinary guidelines are available on the Secretary of State's website or can be mailed to you upon request.

Notary Public Education

All persons are required to take and satisfactorily complete a six-hour course of study approved by the Secretary of State prior to appointment as a notary public. Please note that all persons being appointed, no matter how many commission terms held in the past, are required to take the initial six-hour course of study. (Government Code section 8201(a)(3) and (b))

A notary public who holds a current California notary public commission and who has completed an approved six-hour course at least one time is required to take and satisfactorily complete an approved three-hour refresher course prior to reappointment as a notary public. The three-hour refresher course can only be used to satisfy the education requirement if the notary public is applying for a new commission before their current commission has expired. If the notary public's commission has expired, the individual must satisfactorily complete a six-hour notary public education course before being appointed for another term, even if the individual already once satisfactorily completed an approved six-hour course for a previous commission.

The Secretary of State reviews and approves courses of study. These approved courses include all the material that a person is expected to know to pass the written examination. The Secretary of State compiles a list of all vendors offering an approved course of study. This list is available on the Secretary of State's website or can be mailed to you upon request. (Government Code section 8201.2)

Requirements and Time Limit for Qualifying

Once the commission has been issued, a person has 30 calendar days from the beginning of the term prescribed in the commission to take, subscribe, and file an oath of office and file a $15,000 surety bond with the county clerk's office. The commission does not take effect until the oath and bond are filed with the county clerk's office. The filing must take place in the county where the notary public maintains a principal place of business as shown in the application on file with the Secretary of State. If the oath and bond are not filed within the 30-calendar-day time period, the commission will not be valid, and the person commissioned may not act as a notary public until a new appointment is obtained and the person has properly qualified within the 30-calendar-day time limit. Government Code section 8213(a) permits the filing of completed oaths and bonds by the applicable county clerk by certified mail or other means of physical delivery that provides a receipt. Exceptions are not made to the 30-day filing requirement due to mail service delays, county clerk mail processing delays, or for any other reason. If mailing an oath and bond to the county clerk, sufficient time must be allowed by the newly appointed notary public to ensure timely filing. (Government Code sections 8212 and 8213)

Notary Public Bond

California law requires every notary public to file an official bond in the amount of $15,000. The notary public bond is not an insurance policy for the notary public. The bond is designed only to provide a limited source of funds for paying claims against the notary public. The notary public remains personally liable to the full extent of any damages sustained and may be required to reimburse the bonding company for sums paid by the company because of misconduct or negligence of the notary public. (Government Code sections 8212 to 8214)

Geographic Jurisdiction

A notary public can provide notarial services throughout the State of California. A notary public is not limited to providing services only in the county where the oath and bond are on file. In virtually all of the certificates the notary public is called on to complete, there will be a venue heading such as "State of California, County of _____." The county named in the heading in the notarial certificate is the county where the signer personally appeared before the notary public. (Government Code section 8200)

Acts Constituting the Practice of Law

California notaries public are prohibited from performing any duties that may be construed as the practice of law. Among the acts which constitute the practice of law are the preparation, drafting, or selection or determination of the kind of any legal document, or giving advice in relation to any legal documents or matters. If asked to perform such tasks, a California notary public should decline and refer the requester to an attorney.

Notary Public Seal

Each notary public is required to have and to use a seal. The seal must be kept in a locked and secured area, under the direct and exclusive control of the notary public, and must not be surrendered to an employer upon termination of employment, whether or not the employer paid for the seal, or to any other person.

Because of the legal requirement that the seal be photographically reproducible, the rubber stamp seal is almost universal. However, notaries public may use an embosser seal in addition to the rubber stamp. The legal requirements for a seal are shown below. (Government Code section 8207)

The seal must:

- Be photographically reproducible when affixed to a document;
- Contain the State Seal and the words "Notary Public";
- Contain the name of the notary public as shown on the commission;
- Contain the name of the county where the oath of office and notary public bond are on file;
- Contain the expiration date of the notary public's commission;
- Contain the sequential identification number (commission number) assigned to the notary public, as well as the identification number assigned to the seal manufacturer or vendor; and
- Be circular not over two inches in diameter, or be a rectangular form of not more than one inch in width by two and one-half inches in length, with a serrated or milled edged border.

Many documents that are acknowledged may later be recorded. A document may not be accepted by the recorder if the notary public seal is illegible. Notaries public are cautioned to make sure that the notary public stamp leaves a clear impression. All the elements must be discernible. The seal should not be placed over signatures or over any printed matter on the document. An illegible or improperly placed seal may result in rejection of the document for recordation and result in inconveniences and extra expenses for all those involved.

The law allows a limited exception when a notary public may authenticate an official act without using an official notary public seal. Because subdivision maps usually are drawn on a material that will not accept standard stamp pad ink and other acceptable inks are not as readily available, acknowledgments for California subdivision map certificates may be notarized without the official seal. The notary public's name, the county of the notary public's principal place of business, and the commission expiration date must be typed or printed below or immediately adjacent to the notary public's signature on the acknowledgment. (Government Code section 66436(c))

A NOTARY PUBLIC SHALL NOT USE THE OFFICIAL SEAL OR THE TITLE NOTARY PUBLIC FOR ANY PURPOSE OTHER THAN THE RENDERING OF NOTARIAL SERVICE. (Government Code section 8207)

A notary public is guilty of a misdemeanor if the notary public willfully fails to keep his or her notary public seal under the notary public's direct and exclusive control or if the notary public willfully surrenders the notary public's seal to any person not authorized to possess it. (Government Code section 8228.1)

When the notary public commission is no longer valid, the notary public seal must be destroyed to protect the notary public from possible fraudulent use by another. (Government Code section 8207)

Identification

When completing a certificate of acknowledgment or a jurat, a notary public is required to certify to the identity of the signer of the document. (Civil Code sections 1185(a), 1189, Government Code section 8202) Identity is established if the notary public is presented with satisfactory evidence of the signer's identity. (Civil Code section 1185(a))

Satisfactory Evidence – "Satisfactory Evidence" means the absence of any information, evidence, or other circumstances which would lead a reasonable person to believe that the individual is not the individual he or she claims to be and (A) identification documents or (B) the oath of a single credible witness or (C) the oaths of two credible witnesses under penalty of perjury, as specified below:

A. **Identification Documents** – The notary public can establish the identity of the signer using identification documents as follows (Civil Code section 1185(b)(3) and (4)):

1. There is reasonable reliance on any one of the following forms of identification, provided it is current or was issued within 5 years:

a. An identification card or driver's license issued by the California Department of Motor Vehicles;

b. A United States passport;

c. An inmate identification card issued by the California Department of Corrections and Rehabilitation, if the inmate is in custody in California state prison;

d. Any form of inmate identification issued by a sheriff's department, if the inmate is in custody in a local detention facility; or

2. There is reasonable reliance on any one of the following forms of identification, provided that it also contains a photograph, description of the person, signature of the person, and an identifying number:

(a) A valid consular identification document issued by a consulate from the applicant's country of citizenship, or a valid passport from the applicant's country of citizenship;

(b) A driver's license issued by another state or by a Canadian or Mexican public agency authorized to issue driver's licenses;

(c) An identification card issued by another state;

(d) A United States military identification card (caution: current military identification cards might not contain all the required information);

(e) An employee identification card issued by an agency or office of the State of California, or an agency or office of a city, county, or city and county in California.

(f) An identification card issued by a federally recognized tribal government.

Note: The notary public must include in his or her journal the type of identifying document, the governmental agency issuing the document, the serial or identifying number of the document, and the date of issue or expiration of the document that was used to establish the identity of the signer. (Government Code section 8206(a)(2)(D))

B. **Oath of a Single Credible Witness** – The identity of the signer can be established by the oath of a single credible witness whom the notary public personally knows. (Civil Code section 1185(b)(1)) The notary public must establish the identity of the credible witness by the presentation of paper identification documents as set forth above. Under oath, the credible witness must swear or affirm that each of the following is true (Civil Code section 1185(b)(1) (A)(i)-(v)):

1. The individual appearing before the notary public as the signer of the document is the person named in the document;

2. The credible witness personally knows the signer;

3. The credible witness reasonably believes that the circumstances of the signer are such that it would be very difficult or impossible for the signer to obtain another form of identification;

4. The signer does not possess any of the identification documents authorized by law to establish the signer's identity; and

5. The credible witness does not have a financial interest and is not named in the document signed.

Note: The single credible witness must sign the notary public's journal or the notary public must indicate in his or her journal the type of identifying document, the identifying number of the document, and the date of issuance or expiration of the document presented by the witness to establish the identity of the witness. (Government Code section 8206(a)(2)(D))

C. **Oaths of Two Credible Witnesses** – The identity of the signer can be established by the oaths of two credible witnesses whom the notary public does not personally know. (Civil Code section 1185(b)(2)) The notary public first must establish the identities of the two credible witnesses by the presentation of paper identification documents as listed above. Under oath, the credible witnesses must swear or affirm under penalty of perjury to each of the things sworn to or affirmed by a single credible witness, as set forth above. (Civil Code sections 1185(b)(2) and 1185(b)(1)(A)(i)-(v))

Note: The credible witnesses must sign the notary public's journal and the notary public must indicate in his or her journal the type of identifying documents, the identifying numbers of the documents, and the dates of issuance or expiration of the documents presented by the witnesses to establish their identities. (Government Code section 8206(a)(2)(E))

Notary Public Journal

A notary public is required to keep one active sequential journal at a time of all acts performed as a notary public. The journal must be kept in a locked and secured area (such as a lock box or locked desk drawer), under the direct and exclusive control of the notary public. The journal shall include the items shown below. (Government Code section 8206(a))

- Date, time and type of each official act (e.g., acknowledgment, jurat).
- Character of every instrument sworn to, affirmed, acknowledged or proved before the notary public (e.g., deed of trust).
- The signature of each person whose signature is being notarized.
- A statement that the identity of a person making an acknowledgment or taking an oath or affirmation was based on "satisfactory evidence" pursuant to Civil Code section 1185. If satisfactory evidence was based on:

1. Paper identification, the journal shall contain the type of identifying document, the governmental agency issuing the document, the serial or identifying number of the document, and the date of issue or expiration of the document;

2. A single credible witness personally known to the notary public, the journal shall contain the signature of the credible witness or the type of identifying document, the governmental agency issuing the document, the serial or identifying number of the document, and the date of issue or expiration of the document establishing the identity of the credible witness; or

3. Two credible witnesses whose identities are proven upon the presentation of satisfactory evidence, the journal shall contain the signatures of the credible witnesses and the type of identifying document, the governmental agency issuing the document, the serial or identifying number of the document, and the date of issue or expiration of the document establishing the identity of the credible witnesses.

- The fee charged for the notarial service.
- If the document to be notarized is a deed, quitclaim deed, deed of trust, or other document affecting real property or a power of attorney document, the notary public shall require the party signing the document to place his or her right thumbprint in the journal. If the right thumbprint is not available, then the notary public shall have the party use his or her left thumb, or any available finger and shall so indicate in the journal. If the party signing the document is physically unable to provide a thumb or fingerprint, the notary public shall so indicate in the journal and shall also provide an explanation of that physical condition.

If the sequential journal is stolen, lost, misplaced, destroyed, damaged, or otherwise rendered unusable, the notary public immediately must notify the Secretary of State by certified or registered mail or any other means of physical delivery that provides a receipt. The notification must include the periods of journal entries, the notary public commission number, the commission expiration date, and, when applicable, a photocopy of the police report that lists the journal. (Government Code section 8206(b))

A notary public must respond within 15 business days after the receipt of a written request from any member of the public for a copy of a transaction in the notary public journal by supplying either a photostatic copy of a line item from the notary public's journal or an acknowledgment that no such line item exists. The written request shall include the name of the parties, the type of document, and the month and year in which the document was notarized. The cost to provide the requested information must not exceed thirty cents ($0.30) per page. (Government Code sections 8206(c) and 8206.5)

The sequential journal is the exclusive property of the notary public and shall not be surrendered to an employer upon termination of employment, whether or not the employer paid for the journal, or at any other time. The circumstances in which the notary public must relinquish the journal or permit inspection and copying of journal transactions and the procedures the notary public must follow are specified in Government Code section 8206(d).

A notary public is guilty of a misdemeanor if the notary public willfully fails to properly maintain the notary public's journal. (Government Code section 8228.1)

Within 30 days from the date the notary public commission is no longer valid, the notary public must deliver all notarial journals, records and papers to the county clerk's office where the oath is on file. If the notary public willfully fails or refuses to do so, the notary public is guilty of a misdemeanor, and shall be personally liable for damages to any person injured by that action or inaction. (Government Code section 8209) Any notarial journals, records and papers delivered to the Secretary of State will be returned to the sender.

Conflict of Interest

A notary public may notarize documents for relatives or others, unless doing so would provide a direct financial or beneficial interest to the notary public. Given California's community property law, care should be exercised if notarizing for a spouse or a domestic partner.

A notary public would have a direct financial or beneficial interest to a transaction in the following situations (Government Code section 8224):

- If a notary public is named, individually, as a principal to a financial transaction.
- If a notary public is named, individually, as any of the following to a real property transaction: beneficiary, grantor, grantee, mortgagor, mortgagee, trustor, trustee, vendor, vendee, lessor, or lessee.

A notary public would not have a direct financial or beneficial interest in a transaction if a notary public is acting in the capacity of an agent, employee, insurer, attorney, escrow holder, or lender for a person having a direct financial or beneficial interest in the transaction.

If in doubt as to whether or not to notarize, the notary public should seek the advice of an attorney.

Acknowledgment

The form most frequently completed by the notary public is the certificate of acknowledgment. The certificate of acknowledgment must be in the form set forth in Civil Code section 1189. In the certificate of acknowledgment, the notary public certifies:

- That the signer personally appeared before the notary public on the date indicated in the county indicated;
- To the identity of the signer; and
- That the signer acknowledged executing the document.

The notary public sequential journal must contain a statement that the identity of a person making the acknowledgment or taking the oath or affirmation was based on satisfactory evidence. If identity was established based on the oath of a credible witness personally known to the notary public, then the journal must contain the signature of the credible witness or the type of identifying document used to establish the witness' identity, the governmental agency issuing the document, the serial or identifying number of the document, and the date of issue or expiration of the document. If the identity of the person making the acknowledgment or taking the oath or affirmation was established by the oaths or affirmations of two credible witnesses whose identities are proven to the notary public upon the presentation of satisfactory evidence, then the journal must contain the signatures of the credible witnesses and the type of identifying documents, the identifying numbers of the documents and the dates of issuance or expiration of the documents presented by the witnesses to establish their identities.

The certificate of acknowledgment must be filled completely out at the time the notary public's signature and seal are affixed. The certificate of acknowledgment is executed under penalty of perjury. (Civil Code section 1189(a)(1))

The completion of a certificate of acknowledgment that contains statements that the notary public knows to be false not only may cause the notary public to be liable for civil penalties and administrative action, but is also a criminal offense. The notary public who willfully states as true any material fact known to be false is subject to a civil penalty not exceeding $10,000. (Civil Code section 1189(a)(4))

A notary public may complete a certificate of acknowledgment required in another state or jurisdiction of the United States on documents to be filed in that other state or jurisdiction, provided the form does not require the notary public to determine or certify that the signer holds a particular representative capacity or to make other determinations and certifications not allowed by California law.

Any certificate of acknowledgment taken within this state shall be in the following form:

A notary public or other officer completing this certificate verifies only the identity of the individual who signed the document to which this certificate is attached, and not the truthfulness, accuracy, or validity of that document.

State of California
County of _____ }

    On _____ before me, (here insert name and title of the officer), personally appeared _____
_____
_____
_____ ,

who proved to me on the basis of satisfactory evidence to be the person(s) whose name(s) is/are subscribed to the within instrument and acknowledged to me that he/she/they executed the same in his/her/their authorized capacity(ies), and that by his/her/their signature(s) on the instrument the person(s), or the entity upon behalf of which the person(s) acted, executed the instrument.

I certify under PENALTY OF PERJURY under the laws of the State of California that the foregoing paragraph is true and correct.

WITNESS my hand and official seal.

Notary Public Signature   Notary Public Seal

Note: An acknowledgment cannot be affixed to a document mailed or otherwise delivered to a notary public whereby the signer did not personally appear before the notary public, even if the signer is known by the notary public. Also, a notary public seal and signature cannot be affixed to a document without the correct notarial wording.

Jurat

The second form most frequently completed by a notary public is the jurat. (Government Code section 8202) The jurat is identified by the wording "Subscribed and sworn to (or affirmed)" contained in the form. In the jurat, the notary public certifies:

- That the signer personally appeared before the notary public on the date indicated and in the county indicated;
- That the signer signed the document in the presence of the notary public;
- That the notary public administered the oath or affirmation*; and
- To the identity of the signer.

Any jurat taken within this state shall be in the following form:

> A notary public or other officer completing this certificate verifies only the identity of the individual who signed the document to which this certificate is attached, and not the truthfulness, accuracy, or validity of that document.

State of California
County of _____

Subscribed and sworn to (or affirmed) before me on this _____ day of _____, 20__, by _____, proved to me on the basis of satisfactory evidence to be the person(s) who appeared before me.

Notary Public Signature   Notary Public Seal

Note: A jurat cannot be affixed to a document mailed or otherwise delivered to a notary public whereby the signer did not personally appear, take an oath, and sign in the presence of the notary public, even if the signer is known by the notary public. Also, a notary public seal and signature cannot be affixed to a document without the correct notarial wording.

There is no prescribed wording for the oath, but an acceptable oath would be "Do you swear or affirm that the statements in this document are true?" When administering the oath, the signer and notary public traditionally each raise their right hand but this is not a legal requirement.

Proof of Execution by a Subscribing Witness

If a person, called the principal, has signed a document but does not personally appear before a notary public, another person can appear on the principal's behalf to prove the principal signed (or "executed") the document. That person is called a subscribing witness. (Code of Civil Procedure section 1935)

A proof of execution by a subscribing witness cannot be used in conjunction with any power of attorney, quitclaim deed, grant deed (other than a trustee's deed resulting from a decree of foreclosure, or a nonjudicial foreclosure pursuant to Civil Code section 2924, or to a deed of reconveyance), mortgage, deed of trust, security agreement, any instrument affecting real property, or any instrument requiring a notary public to obtain a thumbprint from the party signing the document in the notary public's journal. (Government Code section 27287 and Civil Code section 1195(b)(1) and (2))

The requirements for proof of execution by a subscribing witness are as follows:

- The subscribing witness must prove (say under oath) that the person who signed the document as a party, the principal, is the person described in the document, and the subscribing witness personally knows the principal (Civil Code section 1197); and
- The subscribing witness must say, under oath, that the subscribing witness saw the principal sign the document or in the presence of the principal heard the principal acknowledge that the principal signed the document (Code of Civil Procedure section 1935 and Civil Code section 1197); and
- The subscribing witness must say, under oath, that the subscribing witness was requested by the principal to sign the document as a witness and that the subscribing witness did so (Code of Civil Procedure section 1935 and Civil Code section 1197); and
- The notary public must establish the identity of the subscribing witness by the oath of a credible witness whom the notary public personally knows and who personally knows the subscribing witness. The credible witness must also present to the notary public any identification document satisfying the requirements for satisfactory evidence as described in Civil Code section 1185(b)(3) or (4) (Civil Code section 1196); and
- The subscribing witness must sign the notary public's official journal. The credible witness must sign the notary public's official journal or the notary public must record in the notary public's official journal the type of identification document presented, the governmental agency issuing the document, the serial number of the document, and the date of issue or expiration of the document. (Government Code section 8206(a)(2)(C) and (D))

Note: The identity of the subscribing witness must be established by the oath of a credible witness who personally knows the subscribing witness and who is known personally by the notary public. In addition, the credible witness must present an identification document satisfying the requirements of Civil Code section 1185(b)(3) or (4).

Because proof of execution by a subscribing witness is not commonly used, the following scenario is provided as an example of how proof by a subscribing witness may be used.

The principal, Paul, wants to have his signature on a document notarized. Paul is in the hospital and cannot appear before a notary public. So Paul asks a longtime friend, Sue, to visit the hospital and act as a subscribing witness. When Sue comes to the hospital, Sue must watch Paul sign the document. If Paul has signed the document prior to Sue's arrival, Paul must say (acknowledge) to Sue that Paul signed the document. Then Paul should ask Sue to sign the document as a subscribing witness, and Sue must do so.

Next, Sue must take the document to a notary public. Sue chooses Nancy Notary as the notary public. Sue must bring a credible witness with her to see Nancy Notary. Sue chooses Carl, a longtime friend, as a credible witness because Carl has worked with Nancy Notary for several years. Therefore, Carl can act as Sue's credible witness.

Sue and Carl appear together before Nancy. Nancy determines Nancy personally knows Carl and also examines Carl's California driver's license to establish Carl's identity. Then Nancy puts Carl under oath. Under oath or affirmation, Carl swears or affirms that Carl personally knows Sue, that Sue is the person who signed the document as a subscribing witness, and Carl does not have a financial interest in the document signed by Paul and subscribed by Sue, and is not named in the document signed by Paul and subscribed by Sue. Then Nancy puts Sue under oath. Under oath or affirmation, Sue swears or affirms Sue personally knows Paul, that Paul is the person described as a party in the document, that Sue watched Paul sign the document or heard Paul acknowledge that Paul signed the document, that Paul requested Sue sign the document as subscribing witness and that Sue did so.

Sue signs Nancy's notary public journal as a subscribing witness. Carl must sign Nancy's notary public journal as a credible witness, or Nancy must record in the notary public journal that Carl presented a California Department of Motor Vehicles driver's license, the license number, and the date the license expires.

Nancy completes Nancy's notary public journal entry. Nancy then completes a proof of execution certificate and attaches the proof of execution certificate to the document. Sue takes the notarized document back to Paul.

A certificate for proof of execution by a subscribing witness shall be in the following form. (Civil Code section 1195)

A notary public or other officer completing this certificate verifies only the identity of the individual who signed the document to which this certificate is attached, and not the truthfulness, accuracy, or validity of that document.

State of California   } ss.
County of _____

On _____ (date), before me,_____ (name and title of officer), personally appeared _____ (name of subscribing witness), proved to me to be the person whose name is subscribed to the within instrument, as a witness thereto, on the oath of _____ (name of credible witness), a credible witness who is known to me and provided a satisfactory identifying document. _____ (name of subscribing witness), being by me duly sworn, said that he/she was present and saw/heard _____ (name[s] of principal[s]), the same person(s) described in and whose name(s) is/are subscribed to the within or attached instrument in his/her/their authorized capacity(ies) as (a) party(ies) thereto, execute or acknowledge executing the same, and that said affiant subscribed his/her name to the within or attached instrument as a witness at the request of _____ (name[s] of principal[s]).
WITNESS my hand and official seal.

Signature   (Seal)

Note: It is not acceptable to affix a notary public seal and signature to a document without the notarial wording.

Signature by Mark

When the signer of an instrument cannot write (sign) his or her name, that person may sign the document by mark. (Civil Code section 14) The requirements for notarizing a signature by mark are as follows:
- The person signing the document by mark must be identified by the notary public by satisfactory evidence. (Civil Code section 1185)
- The signer's mark must be witnessed by two persons who must subscribe their own names as witnesses on the document. One witness should write the person's name next to the person's mark and then the witness should sign his or her name as a witness. The witnesses are only verifying that they witnessed the individual make his or her mark on the document.

A notary public is not required to identify the two persons who witnessed the signing by mark or to have the two witnesses sign the notary public's journal. **Exception**: If the witnesses were acting in the capacity of credible witnesses in establishing the identity of the person signing by mark, then the witnesses' signatures must be entered in the notary public's journal.

- The signer by mark must include his or her mark in the notary public journal. To qualify as a signature, the making of the mark in the notary public journal, must be witnessed by an individual who must write the person's name next to the mark and then sign his or her own name as a witness.

Following is an example of a document executed by signature by mark:

I, Bob Smith, give my power of attorney to Jane Brown to act as my attorney-in-fact on all matters pertaining to the handling of my estate, finances, and investments. This power of attorney is to remain in effect until another document revoking this instrument has been filed of record thereby rendering this instrument null and void.

Date: _Feb. 5, 2013_ Name: _X Bob Smith_ By: _Vicki Jones_
Witness #1

Steve Miller
Witness #2

> A notary public or other officer completing this certificate verifies only the identity of the individual who signed the document to which this certificate is attached, and not the truthfulness, accuracy, or validity of that document.

State of California
County of _Orange_ }

On February 5, 2013, before me, John Doe, a notary public, personally appeared Bob Smith, who proved to me on the basis of satisfactory evidence to be the person(s) whose name(s) is/~~are~~ subscribed to the within instrument and acknowledged to me that he/~~she/~~ ~~they~~ executed the same in his/~~her/their~~ authorized capacity(~~ies~~), and that by his/~~her/their~~ signature(s) on the instrument the person(s), or the entity upon behalf of which the person(s) acted, executed the instrument.

I certify under PENALTY OF PERJURY under the laws of the State of California that the foregoing paragraph is true and correct.

WITNESS my hand and official seal.

Notary Public Signature   Notary Public Seal

Note: A notary public seal and signature cannot be affixed to a document without the correct notarial wording.

Powers of Attorney - Certifying

A notary public can certify copies of powers of attorney. A certified copy of a power of attorney that has been certified by a notary public has the same force and effect as the original power of attorney. (Probate Code section 4307)

A suggested format for the certification is shown below. Other formats with similar wording may also be acceptable.

State of California   }
County of _____

I ___(name of notary public)___, Notary Public, certify that on ___(date)___, I examined the original power of attorney and the copy of the power of attorney. I further certify that the copy is a true and correct copy of the original power of attorney.

Notary Public Signature   Notary Public Seal

Note: A notary public seal and signature cannot be affixed to a document without the correct notarial wording.

Notarization of Incomplete Documents

A notary public may not notarize a document that is incomplete. If presented with a document for notarization, which the notary public knows from his or her experience to be incomplete or is without doubt on its face incomplete, the notary public must refuse to notarize the document. (Government Code section 8205)

Correcting a Notarial Act

There are no provisions in the law that allow for the correction of a completed notarial act. If a notary public discovers an error in a notarial act after completing the act, then the notary public should notarize the signature on the document again. All requirements for notarization are required for the new notarial act, including completing and attaching a new certificate containing the date of the new notarial act and completing a new journal entry.

Certified Copies

A notary public may only certify copies of powers of attorney under Probate Code section 4307 and his or her notary public journal. (Government Code sections 8205(a)(4), 8205(b)(1), and 8206(e))

Certified copies of birth, fetal death, death, and marriage records may be made only by the State Registrar, by duly appointed and acting local registrars during their term of office, and by county recorders. (Health & Safety Code section 103545)

Illegal Advertising

California law requires any non-attorney notary public who advertises notarial services in a language other than English to post a prescribed notice, in English and the other language, that the notary public is not an attorney and cannot give legal advice about immigration or any other legal matters. The notary public also must list the fees set by statute that a notary public may charge for notarial services. In any event, a notary public may not translate into Spanish the term "Notary Public," defined as "notario publico" or "notario," even if the prescribed notice also is posted. A first offense for violation of this law is grounds for the suspension or revocation of a notary public's commission. A second offense is grounds for the permanent revocation of a notary public's commission. (Government Code section 8219.5)

A notary public legally is barred from advertising in any manner whatsoever that he or she is a notary public if the notary public promotes himself or herself as an immigration specialist or consultant. (Government Code section 8223)

Immigration Documents

Contrary to popular belief, there is no prohibition against notarizing immigration documents. However, several laws specifically outline what a notary public can and cannot do. Only an attorney, a representative accredited by the U.S. Department of Justice, or a person who is registered by the California Secretary of State and bonded as an immigration consultant under the Business and Professions Code may assist a client in completing immigration forms. (Business and Professions Code section 22440) A notary public may not charge any individual more than fifteen dollars ($15) for each set of forms, unless the notary public is also an attorney who is rendering professional services as an attorney. (Government Code section 8223)

Confidential Marriage Licenses

A notary public who is interested in obtaining authorization to issue confidential marriage licenses may apply for approval to the county clerk in the county in which the notary public resides. A notary public must not issue a confidential marriage license unless he or she is approved by the county clerk having jurisdiction. The county clerk offers a course of instruction, which a notary public must complete before authorization will be granted. Additionally, in order for a notary public to perform the marriage, he/she must be one of the persons authorized under Family Code sections 400 to 402 (e.g., priest, minister, or rabbi). The county clerk in the county where the notary public resides may or may not approve the authorization to issue confidential marriage licenses. The county clerk should be consulted if the notary public is interested in obtaining approval. (Family Code section 530)

Grounds for Denial, Revocation, or
Suspension of Appointment and Commission

The Secretary of State may refuse to appoint any person as notary public or may revoke or suspend the commission of a notary public for specific reasons. These reasons include but are not limited to: a substantial misstatement or omission in the application; conviction of a felony or a disqualifying criminal conviction; failure to furnish the Secretary of State with certified copies of the notary public journal when requested to do so or to provide information relating to official acts performed by the notary public; charging more than the fee prescribed by law; failure to complete the acknowledgment at the time the notary public's seal and signature are attached to the document; executing a false certificate; failure to submit to the Secretary of State any court ordered money judgment, including restitution; failure to secure the sequential journal or the official seal; willful failure to report the theft or loss of the sequential journal; making a false certificate or writing containing statements known to be false; fraud relating to a deed of trust; improper notarial acts; unlawfully acting as a notary; filing false or forged documents; forgery; grand theft; falsely obtaining personal information; willful failure to provide access to a journal when requested by a peace officer; and illegal advertising. (Government Code sections 8205, 8214.1, 8219.5 and 8223)

In addition, the Secretary of State may deny the notary public application or suspend the notary public commission of a person who has not complied with child or family support obligations. (Family Code section 17520)

Disciplinary Guidelines

The Secretary of State's disciplinary guidelines facilitate due process and maintain consistency in reviewing applications, investigating alleged violations, and implementing administrative actions. (Government Code section 8220)

The disciplinary guidelines assist administrative law judges, attorneys, notaries public, notary public applicants, and others involved in the disciplinary process. The disciplinary guidelines are available on the Secretary of State's website or can be mailed to you upon request.

Fees

Government Code section 8211 specifies the maximum fees that may be charged for notary public services. However, a notary public may decide to charge no fee or an amount that is less than the maximum amount prescribed by law. The charging of a fee and the amount of the fee charged is at the discretion of the notary public or the notary public's employer, provided it does not exceed the maximum fees. The notary public is required to make an entry in the notary public journal even if no fee was charged, such as "no fee" or "0." (Government Code section 8206) **Exceptions:** 1) Pursuant to Government Code section 8203.6, no fees shall be collected by notaries public appointed to military and naval reservations in accordance with 8203.1; 2) Pursuant to Elections Code section 8080, no fee shall be collected by notaries public for verifying any nomination document or circulator's affidavit; 3) Pursuant to Government Code section 6106, no fee shall be collected by a notary public working for a public entity for services rendered in an affidavit, application, or voucher in relation to the securing of a pension; 4) Pursuant to Government Code section 6107, no fee may be charged to a United States military veteran for notarization of an application or a claim for a pension, allotment, allowance, compensation, insurance, or any other veteran's benefit; and 5) Pursuant to Government Code section 8211(d) no fee can be charged to notarize signatures on vote by mail ballot identification envelopes or other voting materials.

In addition, Government Code section 6100 requires any notary public who is appointed to act for and on behalf of certain public agencies, pursuant to Government Code section 8202.5, to charge for all services and remit the fees received to the employing agency. Each fee charged must be entered in the journal.

Note: The maximum fees are as follows.

Service	Description	Maximum Fee
Acknowledgments	Acknowledgment or proof of a deed or other instrument, to include the seal and the writing of the certificate	$15 for each signature
Oaths/Affirmations	Administering an oath or affirmation to one person	$15
Jurats	Executing the jurat including the seal	$15
Deposition Services	All services rendered in connection with taking a deposition -Administering the oath to the witness -Certificate to the deposition	$30 $7 $7
Voting Materials	Notarize signatures on vote by mail ballot identification envelopes or other voting materials	$0
Powers of Attorney	Certifying a copy of a power of attorney under Probate Code section 4307	$15
Veteran's Benefits	United States military veteran's application or claim for a pension, allotment, allowance, compensation, insurance, or any other veteran's benefit (Government Code section 6107)	$0
Immigration Forms	A notary public qualified and bonded as an immigration consultant may enter data, provided by the client, on immigration forms provided by a federal or state agency	$15 per individual for each set of forms

Change of Address

A notary public is required to notify the Secretary of State of any change of business or residence address in writing, by certified mail or any other means of physical delivery that provides a receipt, within 30 days. (Government Code section 8213.5) Willful failure to notify the Secretary of State of a change of address is punishable as an infraction by a fine of not more than $500. (Government Code section 8213.5)

Upon the change of a business address to a new county, a notary public may elect to file a new oath of office and bond in the new county. However, filing a new oath and bond is optional. Once commissioned, a notary public may perform notary public services anywhere in the state. The original oath and bond must be filed in the county where the notary public's principal place of business is located as shown in the application filed with the Secretary of State. Whether or not a county transfer is filed with the new county after the original oath and bond have been filed in the original county is permissive should the notary public move. (Government Code section 8213) There is no fee for the processing of address change notifications with the Secretary of State.

Note: To ensure proper processing, please include the following information when submitting the written address change notification to the Secretary of State:

- Name of the notary public exactly as it appears on the commission certificate;
- Commission number and expiration date of the commission;
- Whether the address change is for the business, residence, and/or for mailing purposes; and
- New business, including business name, residence, and/or mailing address.

Be sure the address change notification is signed and dated by the notary public. The change of address can be submitted in letter form or, for convenience, an address change form is available on the Secretary of State's website or can be mailed to you upon request.

Foreign Language

A notary public can notarize a signature on a document in a foreign language with which the notary public is not familiar, since a notary public's function only relates to the signature and not the contents of the document. The notary public should be able to identify the type of document being notarized for entry in the notary public's journal. If unable to identify the type of document, the notary public must make an entry to that effect in the journal (e.g., "a document in a foreign language"). The notary public should be mindful of the completeness of the document and must not notarize the signature on the document if the document appears to be incomplete. The notary public is responsible for completing the acknowledgment or jurat form. When notarizing a signature on a document, a notary public must be able to communicate with the customer in order for the signer either to swear to or affirm the contents of the affidavit or to acknowledge the execution of the document. An interpreter should not be used, as vital information could be lost in the translation. If a notary public is unable to communicate with a customer, the customer should be referred to a notary public who speaks the customer's language.

Electronic Notarizations

California notaries public are authorized under current law to perform notarizations on documents electronically as long as all the requirements for a traditional paper-based notarial act are met, including the use of a seal for all but two specific documents used in real estate transactions. California law requires a person to appear personally before a notary public to obtain notarial acts like acknowledgments or jurats. This means the party must be physically present before the notary public. A video image or other form of non-physical representation is not a personal appearance in front of a notary public under California State law.

Common Questions and Answers

Q.   **My neighbor of 20 years has asked me to notarize a document for her. Because I have known her all these years, do I still need to ask for proof of her identity?**

A.   Yes. An acknowledgment may not be taken or a jurat executed on the basis of personal knowledge alone. Satisfactory evidence of the signer's identity must be provided and noted in the journal.

Q.   **I am currently a commissioned notary public applying for reappointment without a break in my commission. Am I still required to submit my fingerprints each time I reapply?**

A.   Yes. All notary public applicants, whether or not they have held a previous commission, must submit fingerprints to the California Department of Justice for the purpose of a background check. The Department of Justice will forward fingerprint images to the Federal Bureau of Investigation requesting a federal summary of criminal information that will be provided to the Secretary of State.

Q.   **If a person was convicted of a DUI, petty theft, trespass, or other crimes, will that person be disqualified from becoming a notary public?**

A. The Secretary of State cannot make a determination as to whether or not a person meets the qualifications to become a notary public until a thorough background check has been completed. If you are concerned as to whether you may be disqualified from becoming a notary public based upon past conviction information, please refer to the Secretary of State's *Notary Public Disciplinary Guidelines,* which also include a list of the most common disqualifying convictions. The disciplinary guidelines are available on the Secretary of State's website or can be mailed to you upon request.

Q. **I had a conviction over 25 years ago. Do I still need to disclose this conviction on my application?**

A. Yes. There is no time limit for disclosure of convictions. If you have ever been convicted, including a conviction for a DUI, you must disclose the conviction on your application. Failure to disclose all conviction information on each application for an appointment or reappointment is grounds for denial.

Q. **How soon can I take the test for reappointment if I currently hold a notary public commission?**

A. To avoid a break in commission terms, you should take the exam at least six months prior to the expiration date of your current commission. Test results are valid for one year from the date of the examination. (Title 2, California Code of Regulations, section 20803)

Q. **Will I be required to take an approved course of study each time I apply for reappointment?**

A. Yes. An applicant for notary public who holds a California notary public commission and who has completed the initial six-hour course of study from an approved vendor will be required to complete a three-hour refresher course of study from an approved vendor prior to reappointment as a notary public for all subsequent terms. In order to meet the requirement to take the three-hour refresher course, a person must apply for reappointment before the current commission expires. An applicant whose commission expires before application is made for a new commission must take an approved six-hour course, even if the applicant previously has completed an approved six-hour course. (Government Code section 8201(b)(2))

Q. **I have completed my approved six-hour course of study and received my proof of completion certificate. What do I do with it?**

A. Once you have completed your six-hour course of study from an approved vendor, staple your proof of completion certificate to the application and take both items with you to the exam.

Q. **Can a six-hour notary public education course be taken in place of a three-hour refresher course?**

A. Yes. A six-hour approved notary public education course satisfies the requirement for a three-hour refresher course. A six-hour approved education course always satisfies the education requirement, regardless if you are a new applicant or applying for reappointment.

Q. **What are the requirements for applicants to be eligible to take an approved three-hour refresher education course?**

A. A notary public who has previously completed an approved six-hour notary public education course is eligible to take an approved three-hour refresher course if the notary public has taken the notary public exam and submitted the application at the exam site prior to the expiration date of the current commission.

Q.   **I applied for reappointment prior to the expiration date of my current notary public commission and took an approved three-hour notary public education course, but I failed the notary public exam. What do I do now?**

A.   If you can take the exam again prior to the expiration date of your current commission, the proof of completion certificate from the three-hour course would still be valid. Attach the proof of completion certificate to your application, along with a 2" x 2" color passport photo of yourself and a check for twenty dollars ($20) when you go to the exam site. However, if your commission expires prior to retaking the exam, the three-hour course no longer meets the education requirements and you will need to take an approved six-hour course. You will need to attach the proof of completion certificate from the approved six-hour notary public education course to the application, along with a 2" x 2" color passport photo of yourself and a check for twenty dollars ($20).

Q.   **I did not file my oath and bond on time. What do I do?**

A.   • If you are a new applicant and took an approved six-hour notary public education course, you must attach a current proof of completion certificate to a new application, along with a 2" x 2" color passport photo of yourself and a check for twenty dollars ($20). You will also need to have your fingerprints retaken at a Live Scan site.

  • If you are a notary public seeking reappointment and took an approved three-hour notary public refresher education course, you will still need to take an approved six-hour course. The three-hour course no longer meets the education requirements because your current commission has expired. You will need to attach the proof of completion certificate for the six-hour course to a new application, along with a 2" x 2" color passport photo of yourself and a check for twenty dollars ($20). You will also need to have your fingerprints retaken at a Live Scan site.

  • If you are a notary public seeking reappointment and took an approved six-hour education course, you must attach a current proof of completion certificate to a new application, along with a 2" x 2" color passport photo of yourself and a check for twenty dollars ($20). You will also need to have your fingerprints retaken at a Live Scan site.

Q.   **Where can I get a Live Scan fingerprint form?**

A.   The Live Scan fingerprint form is available on the Secretary of State's website or upon request from the Secretary of State's office.

Q.   **I have completed an approved course of study and taken the exam, but my current commission doesn't expire for another four months. When will I receive my new commission?**

A.   Your notary public commission for reappointment will be issued 30 days prior to the expiration date of your current commission if you have complied with all the requirements to become a notary public.

Q.   **I have changed my business, mailing or home address. What do I do?**

A.   Send the Secretary of State a letter or a change of address form by certified mail or any other means of physical delivery that provides a receipt within 30 days of the change. (Government Code section 8213.5)

Q.   **I have changed my business from one county to another. What do I do?**

A.   Your commission allows you to notarize throughout the State of California, regardless of where your oath and bond are on file. If the location of your business has changed, you are required to send the Secretary of State an address change by certified mail or any other means of physical delivery that provides a receipt within 30 days of the change. If the address change is for your business, please include the business name in your notification. If the address change includes a change of county, you may choose to file a new oath of office and bond in the county to which your business has moved, however, a county transfer is not required. To file a county change, you must request an oath of office form from the Secretary of State. The oath will have the name of your original county; however, you must take and file your oath of office in the new county, checking the county transfer box at the bottom of the oath form. You also must take a new bond or a duplicate of the original bond and file it together with your oath of office in the new county. A certificate of authorization to manufacture a notary public seal will be sent to you once the Secretary of State has received and processed your oath of office filed in the new county. Your stamp must reflect the county where your most recent oath and bond are filed. (Government Code sections 8213 and 8213.5)

Q. Am I required to see the person sign the document at the time I perform the notarization?

A. It depends on the document being notarized. When preparing a jurat, the person requesting the jurat must appear before you, take an oath, and sign the document in your presence. When preparing a certificate of acknowledgment, the document can be executed before the person brings it to you for notarization. In an acknowledgment, the signer must personally appear before you and acknowledge that the signer executed the document, not that the signer executed the document in your presence. For both a jurat and an acknowledgment, the notary public must certify to the identity of the signer. (Civil Code section 1189 and Government Code section 8202)

Q. I lost my stamp or journal. What do I do?

A. Send a letter immediately by certified mail or any other means of physical delivery that provides a receipt to the Secretary of State explaining what happened and, if applicable, a photocopy of a police report. Upon written request, the Secretary of State will send an authorization so you can have a new stamp made. (Government Code sections 8206 and 8207.3(e))

Q. I have changed my name. What do I do?

A. Send a completed name change form to the Secretary of State. Once approved, you will be issued an amended commission that reflects your new name. Next, you will need to file a new oath of office and an amendment to your bond with the county clerk within 30 days from the date the amended commission was issued in order for the name change to take effect. Within 30 days of the filing, you must obtain a new seal that reflects the new name. Once the amended oath and bond are filed, you may no longer use the commission, including the stamp, that was issued in your previous name. If you fail to file your amended oath and bond within the 30-day time limit, the name change will become void and your commission will revert back to the previous name and you will be required to submit another name change application. (Government Code sections 8213 and 8213.6)

Q. I need to request a new certificate of authorization to have a new stamp made. Is there a fee?

A. No. However, you must send the Secretary of State a written request for a certificate of authorization. (Government Code section 8207.3(e))

Q. How do I resign my commission?

A. If you want to resign your commission, send a letter of resignation to the Secretary of State's office; within 30 days deliver all of your notarial journals, records and papers to the county clerk in which your current oath of office is on file; and destroy your seal. (Government Code section 8209)

Q. What parts of my notary public application are public information?

A. Under Government Code section 8201.5, only your name and address may be provided to the general public. All other information provided on a notary public application is confidential.

GOVERNMENT CODE
Notaries Public
(Chapter 3, Division 1, Title 2)

§ 8200.   Appointment and commission; number; jurisdiction

The Secretary of State may appoint and commission notaries public in such number as the Secretary of State deems necessary for the public convenience. Notaries public may act as such notaries in any part of this state.

§ 8201.   Qualifications to be a notary public; proof of course completion; reappointment

(a) Every person appointed as notary public shall meet all of the following requirements:

(1) Be at the time of appointment a legal resident of this state, except as otherwise provided in Section 8203.1.

(2) Be not less than 18 years of age.

(3) For appointments made on or after July 1, 2005, have satisfactorily completed a six-hour course of study approved by the Secretary of State pursuant to Section 8201.2 concerning the functions and duties of a notary public.

(4) Have satisfactorily completed a written examination prescribed by the Secretary of State to determine the fitness of the person to exercise the functions and duties of the office of notary public. All questions shall be based on the law of this state as set forth in the booklet of the laws of California relating to notaries public distributed by the Secretary of State.

(b) (1) Commencing July 1, 2005, each applicant for notary public shall provide satisfactory proof that he or she has completed the course of study required pursuant to paragraph (3) of subdivision (a) prior to approval of his or her appointment as a notary public by the Secretary of State.

(2) Commencing July 1, 2005, an applicant for notary public who holds a California notary public commission, and who has satisfactorily completed the six-hour course of study required pursuant to paragraph (1) at least one time, shall provide satisfactory proof when applying for reappointment as a notary public that he or she has satisfactorily completed a three-hour refresher course of study prior to reappointment as a notary public by the Secretary of State.

§ 8201.1.   Additional qualifications; determination; identification; fingerprints

(a) Prior to granting an appointment as a notary public, the Secretary of State shall determine that the applicant possesses the required honesty, credibility, truthfulness, and integrity to fulfill the responsibilities of the position. To assist in determining the identity of the applicant and whether the applicant has been convicted of a disqualifying crime specified in subdivision (b) of Section 8214.1, the Secretary of State shall require that applicants be fingerprinted.

(b) Applicants shall submit to the Department of Justice fingerprint images and related information required by the department for the purpose of obtaining information as to the existence and content of a record of state and federal convictions and arrests and information as to the existence and content of a record of state and federal arrests for which the department establishes that the person is free on bail, or on his or her recognizance, pending trial or appeal.

(c) The department shall forward the fingerprint images and related information received pursuant to subdivision (a) to the Federal Bureau of Investigation and request a federal summary of criminal information.

(d) The department shall review the information returned from the Federal Bureau of Investigation and compile and disseminate a response to the Secretary of State pursuant to paragraph (1) of subdivision (p) of Section 11105 of the Penal Code.

(e) The Secretary of State shall request from the department subsequent arrest notification service, pursuant to Section 11105.2 of the Penal Code, for each person who submitted information pursuant to subdivision (a).

(f) The department shall charge a fee sufficient to cover the cost of processing the requests described in this section.

§ 8201.2. Review of course of study for notary public; approval of education course of study, violation of regulations; civil penalties

(a) The Secretary of State shall review the course of study proposed by any vendor to be offered pursuant to paragraph (3) of subdivision (a) and paragraph (2) of subdivision (b) of Section 8201. If the course of study includes all material that a person is expected to know to satisfactorily complete the written examination required pursuant to paragraph (4) of subdivision (a) of Section 8201, the Secretary of State shall approve the course of study.

(b) (1) The Secretary of State shall, by regulation, prescribe an application form and adopt a certificate of approval for the notary public education course of study proposed by a vendor.

(2) The Secretary of State may also provide a notary public education course of study.

(c) The Secretary of State shall compile a list of all persons offering an approved course of study pursuant to subdivision (a) and shall provide the list with every booklet of the laws of California relating to notaries public distributed by the Secretary of State.

(d) (1) A person who provides notary public education and violates any of the regulations adopted by the Secretary of State for approved vendors is subject to a civil penalty not to exceed one thousand dollars ($1,000) for each violation and shall be required to pay restitution where appropriate.

(2) The local district attorney, city attorney, or the Attorney General may bring a civil action to recover the civil penalty prescribed pursuant to this subdivision. A public prosecutor shall inform the Secretary of State of any civil penalty imposed under this section.

§ 8201.5. Application form; confidential nature; use of information

The Secretary of State shall require an applicant for appointment and commission as a notary public to complete an application form and submit a photograph of their person as prescribed by the Secretary of State. Information on this form filed by an applicant with the Secretary of State, except for his or her name and address, is confidential and no individual record shall be divulged by an official or employee having access to it to any person other than the applicant, his or her authorized representative, or an employee or officer of the federal government, the state government, or a local agency, as defined in subdivision (b) of Section 6252 of the Government Code, acting in his or her official capacity. That information shall be used by the Secretary of State for the sole purpose of carrying out the duties of this chapter.

§ 8202. Execution of jurat; administration of oath or affirmation to affiant; attachment to affidavit

(a) When executing a jurat, a notary shall administer an oath or affirmation to the affiant and shall determine, from satisfactory evidence as described in Section 1185 of the Civil Code, that the affiant is the person executing the document. The affiant shall sign the document in the presence of the notary.

(b) To any affidavit subscribed and sworn to before a notary, there shall be attached a jurat that includes a notice at the top, in an enclosed box, stating: "A notary public or other officer completing this certificate verifies only the identity of the individual who signed the document to which this certificate is attached, and not the truthfulness, accuracy, or validity of that document." This notice shall be legible.

(c) The physical format of the boxed notice at the top of the jurat required pursuant to subdivision (d) is an example, for purposes of illustration and not limitation, of the physical format of a boxed notice fulfilling the requirements of subdivision (b).

(d) A jurat executed pursuant to this section shall be in the following form:

> A notary public or other officer completing this
> certificate verifies only the identity of the
> individual who signed the document to which this
> certificate is attached, and not the truthfulness,
> accuracy, or validity of that document.

State of California
County of _____
Subscribed and sworn to (or affirmed) before me on this _____ day of _____, 20__, by
_____, proved to me on the basis of satisfactory evidence to be the person(s)
who appeared before me.

    Seal_____
    Signature_____

§ 8202.5. State, county and school district employees; certificates; expenses

The Secretary of State may appoint and commission the number of state, city, county, and public school district employees as notaries public to act for and on behalf of the governmental entity for which appointed which the Secretary of State deems proper. Whenever a notary is appointed and commissioned, a duly authorized representative of the employing governmental entity shall execute a certificate that the appointment is made for the purposes of the employing governmental entity, and whenever the certificate is filed with any state or county officer, no fees shall be charged by the officer for the filing or issuance of any document in connection with the appointment.

The state or any city, county, or school district for which the notary public is appointed and commissioned pursuant to this section may pay from any funds available for its support the premiums on any bond and the cost of any stamps, seals, or other supplies required in connection with the appointment, commission, or performance of the duties of the notary public.

Any fees collected or obtained by any notary public whose documents have been filed without charge and for whom bond premiums have been paid by the employer of the notary public shall be remitted by the notary public to the employing agency which shall deposit the funds to the credit of the fund from which the salary of the notary public is paid.

§ 8202.7. Private employers; agreement to pay premium on bonds and costs of supplies; remission of fees to employer

A private employer, pursuant to an agreement with an employee who is a notary public, may pay the premiums on any bond and the cost of any stamps, seals, or other supplies required in connection with the appointment, commission, or performance of the duties of such notary public. Such agreement may also provide for the remission of fees collected by such notary public to the employer, in which case any fees collected or obtained by such notary public while such agreement is in effect shall be remitted by such notary public to the employer which shall deposit such funds to the credit of the fund from which the compensation of the notary public is paid.

§ 8202.8. Private employers; limitation on provision of notarial services

Notwithstanding any other provision of law, a private employer of a notary public who has entered into an agreement with his or her employee pursuant to Section 8202.7 may limit, during the employee's ordinary course of employment, the providing of notarial services by the employee solely to transactions directly associated with the business purposes of the employer.

§ 8203.1.   Military and naval reservations; appointment and commission of notaries; qualifications

The Secretary of State may appoint and commission notaries public for the military and naval reservations of the Army, Navy, Coast Guard, Air Force, and Marine Corps of the United States, wherever located in the state; provided, however, that the appointee shall be a citizen of the United States, not less than 18 years of age, and must meet the requirements set forth in paragraphs (3) and (4) of subdivision (a) of Section 8201.

§ 8203.2.   Military and naval reservations, recommendation of commanding officer; jurisdiction of notary

Such notaries public shall be appointed only upon the recommendation of the commanding officer of the reservation in which they are to act, and they shall be authorized to act only within the boundaries of this reservation.

§ 8203.3.   Military and naval reservations, qualifications of notaries

In addition to the qualifications established in Section 8203.1, appointment will be made only from among those persons who are federal civil service employees at the reservation in which they will act as notaries public.

§ 8203.4.   Military and naval reservations; term of office; termination; resignation

The term of office shall be as set forth in Section 8204, except that the appointment shall terminate if the person shall cease to be employed as a federal civil service employee at the reservation for which appointed. The commanding officer of the reservation shall notify the Secretary of State of termination of employment at the reservation for which appointed within 30 days of such termination. A notary public whose appointment terminates pursuant to this section will have such termination treated as a resignation.

§ 8203.5.   Military and naval reservations, jurat

In addition to the name of the State, the jurat shall also contain the name of the reservation in which the instrument is executed.

§ 8203.6.   Military and naval reservations, fees

No fees shall be collected by such notaries public for service rendered within the reservation in the capacity of a notary public.

§ 8204.   Term of office

The term of office of a notary public is for four years commencing with the date specified in the commission.

§ 8204.1.   Cancellation of Commission; failure to pay; notice

The Secretary of State may cancel the commission of a notary public if a check or other remittance accepted as payment for the examination, application, commission, and fingerprint fee is not paid upon presentation to the financial institution upon which the check or other remittance was drawn. Upon receiving written notification that the item presented for payment has not been honored for payment, the Secretary of State shall first give a written notice of the applicability of this section to the notary public or the person submitting the instrument. Thereafter, if the amount is not paid by a cashier's check or the equivalent, the Secretary of State shall give a second written notice of cancellation and the cancellation shall thereupon be effective. This second notice shall be given at least 20 days after the first notice, and no more than 90 days after the commencement date of the commission.

§ 8205.   Duties

(a) It is the duty of a notary public, when requested:

(1) To demand acceptance and payment of foreign and inland bills of exchange, or promissory notes, to protest them for nonacceptance and nonpayment, and, with regard only to the nonacceptance or nonpayment of bills and notes, to exercise any other powers and duties that by the law of nations and according to commercial usages, or by the laws of any other

state, government, or country, may be performed by a notary. This paragraph applies only to a notary public employed by a financial institution, during the course and scope of the notary's employment with the financial institution.

(2) To take the acknowledgment or proof of advance health care directives, powers of attorney, mortgages, deeds, grants, transfers, and other instruments of writing executed by any person, and to give a certificate of that proof or acknowledgment, endorsed on or attached to the instrument. The certificate shall be signed by the notary public in the notary public's own handwriting. A notary public may not accept any acknowledgment or proof of any instrument that is incomplete.

(3) To take depositions and affidavits, and administer oaths and affirmations, in all matters incident to the duties of the office, or to be used before any court, judge, officer, or board. Any deposition, affidavit, oath, or affirmation shall be signed by the notary public in the notary public's own handwriting.

(4) To certify copies of powers of attorney under Section 4307 of the Probate Code. The certification shall be signed by the notary public in the notary public's own handwriting.

(b) It shall further be the duty of a notary public, upon written request:

(1) To furnish to the Secretary of State certified copies of the notary's journal.

(2) To respond within 30 days of receiving written requests sent by certified mail or any other means of physical delivery that provides a receipt from the Secretary of State's office for information relating to official acts performed by the notary.

§ 8206. Sequential journal; contents; thumbprint; loss of journal; copies of pages; exclusive property of notary public; limitations on surrender

(a) (1) A notary public shall keep one active sequential journal at a time, of all official acts performed as a notary public. The journal shall be kept in a locked and secured area, under the direct and exclusive control of the notary. Failure to secure the journal shall be cause for the Secretary of State to take administrative action against the commission held by the notary public pursuant to Section 8214.1.

(2) The journal shall be in addition to, and apart from, any copies of notarized documents that may be in the possession of the notary public and shall include all of the following:

(A) Date, time, and type of each official act.

(B) Character of every instrument sworn to, affirmed, acknowledged, or proved before the notary.

(C) The signature of each person whose signature is being notarized.

(D) A statement as to whether the identity of a person making an acknowledgment or taking an oath or affirmation was based on satisfactory evidence. If identity was established by satisfactory evidence pursuant to Section 1185 of the Civil Code, the journal shall contain the signature of the credible witness swearing or affirming to the identity of the individual or the type of identifying document, the governmental agency issuing the document, the serial or identifying number of the document, and the date of issue or expiration of the document.

(E) If the identity of the person making the acknowledgment or taking the oath or affirmation was established by the oaths or affirmations of two credible witnesses whose identities are proven to the notary public by presentation of any document satisfying the requirements of paragraph (3) or (4) of subdivision (b) of Section 1185 of the Civil Code, the notary public shall record in the journal the type of documents identifying the witnesses, the identifying numbers on the documents identifying the witnesses, and the dates of issuance or expiration of the documents identifying the witnesses.

(F) The fee charged for the notarial service.

(G) If the document to be notarized is a deed, quitclaim deed, deed of trust, or other document affecting real property, or a power of attorney document, the notary public shall require the party signing the document to place his or her right thumbprint in the journal. If the right thumbprint is not available, then the notary shall have the party use his or her left thumb, or any available finger and shall so indicate in the journal. If the party signing the document is physically unable to provide a thumbprint or fingerprint, the notary shall so indicate in the journal and shall also provide an explanation of that physical condition. This paragraph shall not apply to a trustee's deed resulting from a decree of foreclosure or a nonjudicial foreclosure pursuant to Section 2924 of the Civil Code, nor to a deed of reconveyance.

(b) If a sequential journal of official acts performed by a notary public is stolen, lost, misplaced, destroyed, damaged, or otherwise rendered unusable as a record of notarial acts and information, the notary public shall immediately notify the Secretary of State by certified or registered mail or any other means of physical delivery that provides a receipt. The notification shall include the period of the journal entries, the notary public commission number, and the expiration date of the commission, and when applicable, a photocopy of any police report that specifies the theft of the sequential journal of official acts.

(c) Upon written request of any member of the public, which request shall include the name of the parties, the type of document, and the month and year in which notarized, the notary shall supply a photostatic copy of the line item representing the requested transaction at a cost of not more than thirty cents ($0.30) per page.

(d) The journal of notarial acts of a notary public is the exclusive property of that notary public, and shall not be surrendered to an employer upon termination of employment, whether or not the employer paid for the journal, or at any other time. The notary public shall not surrender the journal to any other person, except the county clerk, pursuant to Section 8209, or immediately, or if the journal is not present then as soon as possible, upon request to a peace officer investigating a criminal offense who has reasonable suspicion to believe the journal contains evidence of a criminal offense, as defined in Sections 830.1, 830.2, and 830.3 of the Penal Code, acting in his or her official capacity and within his or her authority. If the peace officer seizes the notary journal, he or she must have probable cause as required by the laws of this state and the United States. A peace officer or law enforcement agency that seizes a notary journal shall notify the Secretary of State by facsimile within 24 hours, or as soon as possible thereafter, of the name of the notary public whose journal has been seized. The notary public shall obtain a receipt for the journal, and shall notify the Secretary of State by certified mail any other means of physical delivery that provides a receipt within 10 days that the journal was relinquished to a peace officer. The notification shall include the period of the journal entries, the commission number of the notary public, the expiration date of the commission, and a photocopy of the receipt. The notary public shall obtain a new sequential journal. If the journal relinquished to a peace officer is returned to the notary public and a new journal has been obtained, the notary public shall make no new entries in the returned journal. A notary public who is an employee shall permit inspection and copying of journal transactions by a duly designated auditor or agent of the notary public's employer, provided that the inspection and copying is done in the presence of the notary public and the transactions are directly associated with the business purposes of the employer. The notary public, upon the request of the employer, shall regularly provide copies of all transactions that are directly associated with the business purposes of the employer, but shall not be required to provide copies of any transaction that is unrelated to the employer's business. Confidentiality and safekeeping of any copies of the journal provided to the employer shall be the responsibility of that employer.

(e) The notary public shall provide the journal for examination and copying in the presence of the notary public upon receipt of a subpoena duces tecum or a court order, and shall certify those copies if requested.

(f) Any applicable requirements of, or exceptions to, state and federal law shall apply to a peace officer engaged in the search or seizure of a sequential journal.

§ 8206.5. Notaries; supplying photostatic copies on request; defending position in a disciplinary proceeding

Upon receiving a request for a copy of a transaction pursuant to subdivision (c) of Section 8206, the notary shall respond to the request within 15 business days after receipt of the request and either supply the photostatic copy requested or acknowledge that no such line item exists. In a disciplinary proceeding for noncompliance with subdivision (c) of Section 8206 or this section, a notary may defend his or her delayed action on the basis of unavoidable, exigent business or personal circumstances.

§ 8207. Seal

A notary public shall provide and keep an official seal, which shall clearly show, when embossed, stamped, impressed or affixed to a document, the name of the notary, the State Seal, the words "Notary Public," and the name of the county wherein the bond and oath of office are filed, and the date the notary public's commission expires. The seal of every notary public commissioned on or after January 1, 1992, shall contain the sequential identification number assigned to the notary and the sequential identification number assigned to the manufacturer or vendor. The notary public shall authenticate with the official seal all official acts.

A notary public shall not use the official notarial seal except for the purpose of carrying out the duties and responsibilities as set forth in this chapter. A notary public shall not use the title "notary public" except for the purpose of rendering notarial service.

The seal of every notary public shall be affixed by a seal press or stamp that will print or emboss a seal which legibly reproduces under photographic methods the required elements of the seal. The seal may be circular not over two inches in diameter, or may be a rectangular form of not more than one inch in width by two and one-half inches in length, with a serrated or milled edged border, and shall contain the information required by this section.

The seal shall be kept in a locked and secured area, under the direct and exclusive control of the notary. Failure to secure the seal shall be cause for the Secretary of State to take administrative action against the commission held by the notary public pursuant to Section 8214.1.

The official seal of a notary public is the exclusive property of that notary public, and shall not be surrendered to an employer upon the termination of employment, whether or not the employer paid for the seal, or to any other person. The notary, or his or her representative, shall destroy or deface the seal upon termination, resignation, or revocation of the notary's commission.

This section shall become operative on January 1, 1992.

§ 8207.1. Identification number

The Secretary of State shall assign a sequential identification number to each notary which shall appear on the notary commission.

This section shall become operative on January 1, 1992.

§ 8207.2. Manufacture, duplication, and sale of seal or stamp; procedures and guidelines for issuance of seals; certificate of authorization

(a) No notary seal or press stamp shall be manufactured, duplicated, sold, or offered for sale unless authorized by the Secretary of State.

(b) The Secretary of State shall develop and implement procedures and guidelines for the issuance of notary seals on or before January 1, 1992.

(c) The Secretary of State shall issue a permit with a sequential identification number to each manufacturer or vendor authorized to issue notary seals. The Secretary of State may establish a fee for the issuance of the permit which shall not exceed the actual costs of issuing the permit.

(d) The Secretary of State shall develop a certificate of authorization to purchase a notary stamp from an authorized vendor.

(e) The certificate of authorization shall be designed to prevent forgeries and shall contain a sequential identification number.

(f) This section shall become operative on January 1, 1992.

§ 8207.3. Certificates of authorization; authorization to provide seal; lost, misplaced, damaged or otherwise unworkable seal

(a) The Secretary of State shall issue certificates of authorization with which a notary public can obtain an official notary seal.

(b) A vendor or manufacturer is authorized to provide a notary with an official seal only upon presentation by the notary public of a certificate of authorization.

(c) A vendor of official seals shall note the receipt of certificates of authorization and sequential identification numbers of certificates presented by a notary public upon a certificate of authorization.

(d) A copy of a certificate of authorization shall be retained by a vendor and the original, which shall contain a sample impression of the seal issued to the notary public, shall be submitted to the Secretary of State for verification and recordkeeping. The Secretary of State shall develop guidelines for submitting certificates of authorization by vendors.

(e) Any notary whose official seal is lost, misplaced, destroyed, broken, damaged, or is rendered otherwise unworkable shall immediately mail or deliver written notice of that fact to the Secretary of State. The Secretary of State, within five working days after receipt of the notice, if requested by a notary, shall issue a certificate of authorization which a notary may use to obtain a replacement seal.

(f) This section shall become operative on January 1, 1992.

§ 8207.4. Violations; penalties

(a) Any person who willfully violates any part of Section 8207.1, 8207.2, 8207.3, or 8207.4 shall be subject to a civil penalty not to exceed one thousand five hundred dollars ($1,500) for each violation, which may be recovered in a civil action brought by the Attorney General or the district attorney or city attorney, or by a city prosecutor in any city and county.

(b) The penalty provided by this section is not an exclusive remedy, and does not affect any other relief or remedy provided by law.

(c) This section shall become operative on January 1, 1992.

§ 8208. Protest of bill or note for nonacceptance or nonpayment

The protest of a notary public acting in the course and scope of employment by a financial institution, under his or her hand and official seal, of a bill of exchange or promissory note for nonacceptance or nonpayment, specifying any of the following is prima facie evidence of the facts recited therein:

(a) The time and place of presentment.

(b) The fact that presentment was made and the manner thereof.

(c) The cause or reason for protesting the bill.

(d) The demand made and the answer given, if any, or the fact that the drawee or acceptor could not be found.

§ 8209. Resignation, disqualification or removal of notary; records delivered to clerk; misdemeanor; death; destruction of records

(a) If any notary public resigns, is disqualified, removed from office, or allows his or her appointment to expire without obtaining reappointment within 30 days, all notarial records and papers shall be delivered within 30 days to the clerk of the county in which the notary public's current official oath of office is on file. If the notary public willfully fails or refuses to deliver all notarial records and papers to the county clerk within 30 days, the person is guilty of a misdemeanor and shall be personally liable for damages to any person injured by that action or inaction.

(b) In the case of the death of a notary public, the personal representative of the deceased shall promptly notify the Secretary of State of the death of the notary public and shall deliver all notarial records and papers of the deceased to the clerk of the county in which the notary public's official oath of office is on file.

(c) After 10 years from the date of deposit with the county clerk, if no request for, or reference to such records has been made, they may be destroyed upon order of court.

§ 8211. Fees

Fees charged by a notary public for the following services shall not exceed the fees prescribed by this section.

(a) For taking an acknowledgment or proof of a deed, or other instrument, to include the seal and the writing of the certificate, the sum of fifteen dollars ($15) for each signature taken.

(b) For administering an oath or affirmation to one person and executing the jurat, including the seal, the sum of fifteen dollars ($15).

(c) For all services rendered in connection with the taking of any deposition, the sum of thirty dollars ($30), and in addition thereto, the sum of seven dollars ($7) for administering the oath to the witness and the sum of seven dollars ($7) for the certificate to the deposition.

(d) No fee may be charged to notarize signatures on vote by mail ballot identification envelopes or other voting materials.

(e) For certifying a copy of a power of attorney under Section 4307 of the Probate Code the sum of fifteen dollars ($15).

(f) In accordance with Section 6107, no fee may be charged to a United States military veteran for notarization of an application or a claim for a pension, allotment, allowance, compensation, insurance, or any other veteran's benefit.

§ 8212. Bond; amount; form

Every person appointed a notary public shall execute an official bond in the sum of fifteen thousand dollars ($15,000). The bond shall be in the form of a bond executed by an admitted surety insurer and not a deposit in lieu of bond.

§ 8213. Bonds and oaths; filing; certificate; copy of oath as evidence; transfer to new county; name changes; fees

(a) No later than 30 days after the beginning of the term prescribed in the commission, every person appointed a notary public shall file an official bond and an oath of office in the office of the county clerk of the county within which the person maintains a principal place of business as shown in the application submitted to the Secretary of State, and the commission shall not take effect unless this is done within the 30-day period. A person appointed to be a notary public shall take and subscribe the oath of office either in the office of that county clerk or before another notary public in that county. If the oath of office is taken and subscribed before the county clerk, the person appointed to be a notary public shall present an identification document meeting the requirements of subparagraph (A) or (B) of paragraph (3), or of subparagraph (A) or (E) or paragraph (4), of subdivision (b) of Section 1185 of the Civil Code to the county clerk as satisfactory evidence of identity. If the oath of office is taken and subscribed before a notary public, the oath and bond may be filed with the county clerk by certified mail or any other means of physical delivery that provides a receipt. Upon the filing of the oath and bond, the county clerk shall immediately transmit to the Secretary of State a certificate setting forth the fact of the filing and containing a copy of the official oath, personally signed by the notary public in the form set forth in the commission and shall immediately deliver the bond to the county recorder for recording. The county clerk shall retain the oath of office for one year following the expiration of the term of the commission for which the oath was taken, after which the oath may be destroyed or otherwise disposed of. The copy of the oath, personally signed by the notary public, on file with the Secretary of State may at any time be read in evidence with like effect as the original oath, without further proof.

(b) If a notary public transfers the principal place of business from one county to another, the notary public may file a new oath of office and bond, or a duplicate of the original bond with the county clerk to which the principal place of business was transferred. If the notary public elects to make a new filing, the notary public shall, within 30 days of the filing, obtain an official seal which shall include the name of the county to which the notary public has transferred. In a case where the notary public elects to make a new filing, the same filing and recording fees are applicable as in the case of the original filing and recording of the bond.

(c) If a notary public submits an application for a name change to the Secretary of State, the notary public shall, within 30 days from the date an amended commission is issued, file a new oath of office and an amendment to the bond with the county clerk in which the principal place of business is located. The amended commission with the name change shall not take effect unless the filing is completed within the 30-day period. The amended commission with the name change takes effect the date the oath and amendment to the bond is filed with the county clerk. If the principal place of business address was changed in the application for name change, either a new or duplicate of the original bond shall be filed with the county clerk with the amendment to the bond. The notary public shall, within 30 days of the filing, obtain an official seal that includes the name of the notary public and the name of the county to which the notary public has transferred, if applicable.

(d) The recording fee specified in Section 27361 of the Government Code shall be paid by the person appointed a notary public. The fee may be paid to the county clerk who shall transmit it to the county recorder.

(e) The county recorder shall record the bond and shall thereafter mail, unless specified to the contrary, it to the person named in the instrument and, if no person is named, to the party leaving it for recording.

§ 8213.5.   Change in location or address of business or residence; notice

A notary public shall notify the Secretary of State by certified mail or any other means of physical delivery that provides a receipt within 30 days as to any change in the location or address of the principal place of business or residence. A notary public shall not use a commercial mail receiving agency or post office box as his or her principal place of business or residence, unless the notary public also provides the Secretary of State with a physical street address as the principal place of residence. Willful failure to notify the Secretary of State of a change of address shall be punishable as an infraction by a fine of not more than five hundred dollars ($500).

§ 8213.6.   Name changes; application; filing

If a notary public changes his or her name, the notary public shall complete an application for name change form and file that application with the Secretary of State. Information on this form shall be subject to the confidentiality provisions described in Section 8201.5. Upon approval of the name change form, the Secretary of State shall issue a commission that reflects the new name of the notary public. The term of the commission and commission number shall remain the same. Willful failure to notify the Secretary of State of a name change shall be punishable as an infraction by a fine of not more than five hundred dollars ($500).

§ 8214.   Misconduct or neglect

For the official misconduct or neglect of a notary public, the notary public and the sureties on the notary public's official bond are liable in a civil action to the persons injured thereby for all the damages sustained.

§ 8214.1.   Grounds for refusal, revocation or suspension of commission

The Secretary of State may refuse to appoint any person as notary public or may revoke or suspend the commission of any notary public upon any of the following grounds:

(a) Substantial and material misstatement or omission in the application submitted to the Secretary of State to become a notary public.

(b) Conviction of a felony, a lesser offense involving moral turpitude, or a lesser offense of a nature incompatible with the duties of a notary public. A conviction after a plea of nolo contendere is deemed to be a conviction within the meaning of this subdivision.

(c) Revocation, suspension, restriction, or denial of a professional license, if the revocation, suspension, restriction, or denial was for misconduct based on dishonesty, or for any cause substantially relating to the duties or responsibilities of a notary public.

(d) Failure to discharge fully and faithfully any of the duties or responsibilities required of a notary public.

(e) When adjudicated liable for damages in any suit grounded in fraud, misrepresentation, or for a violation of the state regulatory laws, or in any suit based upon a failure to discharge fully and faithfully the duties as a notary public.

(f) The use of false or misleading advertising wherein the notary public has represented that the notary public has duties, rights, or privileges that he or she does not possess by law.

(g) The practice of law in violation of Section 6125 of the Business and Professions Code.

(h) Charging more than the fees prescribed by this chapter.

(i) Commission of any act involving dishonesty, fraud, or deceit with the intent to substantially benefit the notary public or another, or substantially injure another.

(j) Failure to complete the acknowledgment at the time the notary's signature and seal are affixed to the document.

(k) Failure to administer the oath or affirmation as required by paragraph (3) of subdivision (a) of Section 8205.

(l) Execution of any certificate as a notary public containing a statement known to the notary public to be false.

(m) Violation of Section 8223.

(n) Failure to submit any remittance payable upon demand by the Secretary of State under this chapter or failure to satisfy any court-ordered money judgment, including restitution.

(o) Failure to secure the sequential journal of official acts, pursuant to Section 8206, or the official seal, pursuant to Section 8207, or willful failure to report the theft or loss of the sequential journal, pursuant to subdivision (b) of Section 8206.

(p) Violation of Section 8219.5.

(q) Commission of an act in violation of Section 6203, 8214.2, 8225, or 8227.3 of the Government Code or of Section 115, 470, 487, subdivision (a) of Section 487a, or Section 530.5 of the Penal Code.

(r) Willful failure to provide access to the sequential journal of official acts upon request by a peace officer.

§ 8214.15. Civil penalties

(a) In addition to any commissioning or disciplinary sanction, a violation of subdivision (f), (i), (l), (m), or (p) of Section 8214.1, or a willful violation of subdivision (d) of Section 8214.1, is punishable by a civil penalty not to exceed one thousand five hundred dollars ($1,500).

(b) In addition to any commissioning or disciplinary sanction, a violation of subdivision (h), (j), or (k) of Section 8214.1, or a negligent violation of subdivision (d) of Section 8214.1 is punishable by a civil penalty not to exceed seven hundred fifty dollars ($750).

(c) The civil penalty may be imposed by the Secretary of State if a hearing is not requested pursuant to Section 8214.3. If a hearing is requested, the hearing officer shall make the determination.

(d) Any civil penalties collected pursuant to this section shall be transferred to the General Fund. It is the intent of the Legislature that to the extent General Fund moneys are raised by penalties collected pursuant to this section, that money shall be made available to the Secretary of State's office to defray its costs of investigating and pursuing commissioning and monetary remedies for violations of the notary public law.

§ 8214.2. Fraud relating to deed of trust; single-family residence; felony

(a) A notary public who knowingly and willfully with intent to defraud performs any notarial act in relation to a deed of trust on real property consisting of a single-family residence containing not more than four dwelling units, with knowledge that the deed of trust contains any false statements or is forged, in whole or in part, is guilty of a felony.

(b) The penalty provided by this section is not an exclusive remedy and does not affect any other relief or remedy provided by law.

§ 8214.21. Failure to provide access to the sequential journal of notarial acts; civil penalties

A notary public who willfully fails to provide access to the sequential journal of notarial acts when requested by a peace officer shall be subject to a civil penalty not exceeding two thousand five hundred dollars ($2,500). An action to impose a civil penalty under this subdivision may be brought by the Secretary of State in an administrative proceeding or any public prosecutor in superior court, and shall be enforced as a civil judgment. A public prosecutor shall inform the secretary of any civil penalty imposed under this section.

§ 8214.23. Failure to obtain thumbprint; civil penalties; limitations

(a) A notary public who fails to obtain a thumbprint, as required by Section 8206, from a party signing a document shall be subject to a civil penalty not exceeding two thousand five hundred dollars ($2,500). An action to impose a civil penalty under this subdivision may be brought by the Secretary of State in an administrative proceeding or any public prosecutor in superior court, and shall be enforced as a civil judgment. A public prosecutor shall inform the secretary of any civil penalty imposed under this section.

(b) Not withstanding any other limitation of time described in Section 802 of the Penal Code, or any other provision of law, prosecution for a violation of this offense shall be commenced within four years after discovery of the commission of the offense, or within four years after the completion of the offense, whichever is later.

§ 8214.3. Hearing prior to denial or revocation of commission or imposition of civil penalties; law governing; exceptions

Prior to a revocation or suspension pursuant to this chapter or after a denial of a commission, or prior to the imposition of a civil penalty, the person affected shall have a right to a hearing on the matter and the proceeding shall be conducted in accordance with Chapter 5 (commencing with Section 11500) of Part 1 of Division 3, except that a person shall not have a right to a hearing after a denial of an application for a notary public commission in either of the following cases:

(a) The Secretary of State has, within one year previous to the application, and after proceedings conducted in accordance with Chapter 5 (commencing with Section 11500) of Part 1 of Division 3, denied or revoked the applicant's application or commission.

(b) The Secretary of State has entered an order pursuant to Section 8214.4 finding that the applicant has committed or omitted acts constituting grounds for suspension or revocation of a notary public's commission.

§ 8214.4. Resignation or expiration of commission not a bar to investigation or disciplinary proceedings

Notwithstanding this chapter or Chapter 5 (commencing with Section 11500) of Part 1 of Division 3, if the Secretary of State determines, after proceedings conducted in accordance with Chapter 5 (commencing with Section 11500) of Part 1 of Division 3, that any notary public has committed or omitted acts constituting grounds for suspension or revocation of a notary public's commission, the resignation or expiration of the notary public's commission shall not bar the Secretary of State from instituting or continuing an investigation or instituting disciplinary proceedings. Upon completion of the disciplinary proceedings, the Secretary of

State shall enter an order finding the facts and stating the conclusion that the facts would or would not have constituted grounds for suspension or revocation of the commission if the commission had still been in effect.

§ 8214.5. Revocation of commission; filing copy with county clerk

Whenever the Secretary of State revokes the commission of any notary public, the Secretary of State shall file with the county clerk of the county in which the notary public's principal place of business is located a copy of the revocation. The county clerk shall note such revocation and its date upon the original record of such certificate.

§ 8214.8. Revocation upon certain convictions

Upon conviction of any offense in this chapter, or of Section 6203, or of any felony, of a person commissioned as a notary public, in addition to any other penalty, the court shall revoke the commission of the notary public, and shall require the notary public to surrender to the court the seal of the notary public. The court shall forward the seal, together with a certified copy of the judgment of conviction, to the Secretary of State.

§ 8216. Release of surety

When a surety of a notary desires to be released from responsibility on account of future acts, the release shall be pursuant to Article 11 (commencing with Section 996.110), and not by cancellation or withdrawal pursuant to Article 13 (commencing with Section 996.310), of Chapter 2 of Title 14 of Part 2 of the Code of Civil Procedure. For this purpose the surety shall make application to the superior court of the county in which the notary public's principal place of business is located and the copy of the application and notice of hearing shall be served on the Secretary of State as the beneficiary.

§ 8219.5. Advertising in language other than English; posting of notice relating to legal advice and fees; translation of notary public into Spanish; suspension

(a) Every notary public who is not an attorney who advertises the services of a notary public in a language other than English by signs or other means of written communication, with the exception of a single desk plaque, shall post with that advertisement a notice in English and in the other language which sets forth the following:

(1) This statement: I am not an attorney and, therefore, cannot give legal advice about immigration or any other legal matters.

(2) The fees set by statute which a notary public may charge.

(b) The notice required by subdivision (a) shall be printed and posted as prescribed by the Secretary of State.

(c) Literal translation of the phrase "notary public" into Spanish, hereby defined as "notario publico" or "notario," is prohibited. For purposes of this subdivision, "literal translation" of a word or phrase from one language to another means the translation of a word or phrase without regard to the true meaning of the word or phrase in the language which is being translated.

(d) The Secretary of State shall suspend for a period of not less than one year or revoke the commission of any notary public who fails to comply with subdivision (a) or (c). However, on the second offense the commission of such notary public shall be revoked permanently.

§ 8220. Rules and regulations

The Secretary of State may adopt rules and regulations to carry out the provisions of this chapter.

The regulations shall be adopted in accordance with the Administrative Procedure Act (Chapter 3.5 (commencing with Section 11340) of Part 1 of Division 3).

§ 8221. Destruction, defacement or concealment of records or papers; misdemeanor; liability for damages

(a) If any person shall knowingly destroy, deface, or conceal any records or papers belonging to the office of a notary public, such person shall be guilty of a misdemeanor and be liable in a civil action for damages to any person injured as a result of such destruction, defacing, or concealment.

(b) Notwithstanding any other limitation of time described in Section 802 of the Penal Code, or any other provision of law, prosecution for a violation of this offense shall be commenced within four years after discovery of the commission of the offense, or within four years after the completion of the offense, whichever is later.

(c) The penalty provided by this section is not an exclusive remedy and does not affect any other relief or remedy provided by law.

§ 8222. Injunction; reimbursement for expenses

(a) Whenever it appears to the Secretary of State that any person has engaged or is about to engage in any acts or practices which constitute or will constitute a violation of any provision of this chapter or any rule or regulation prescribed under the authority thereof, the Secretary of State may apply for an injunction, and upon a proper showing, any court of competent jurisdiction has power to issue a permanent or temporary injunction or restraining order to enforce the provisions of this chapter, and any party to the action has the right to prosecute an appeal from the order or judgment of the court.

(b) The court may order a person subject to an injunction or restraining order provided for in this section to reimburse the Secretary of State for expenses incurred in the investigation related to the petition. The Secretary of State shall refund any amount received as reimbursement should the injunction or restraining order be dissolved by an appellate court.

§ 8223. Notary public with expertise in immigration matters; advertising status as notary public; entry of information on forms; fee limitations

(a) A notary public who holds himself or herself out as being an immigration specialist, immigration consultant, or any other title or description reflecting an expertise in immigration matters shall not advertise in any manner whatsoever that he or she is a notary public.

(b) A notary public qualified and bonded as an immigration consultant under Chapter 19.5 (commencing with Section 22440) of Division 8 of the Business and Professions Code may enter data, provided by the client, on immigration forms provided by a federal or state agency. The fee for this service shall not exceed fifteen dollars ($15) per individual for each set of forms. If notary services are performed in relation to the set of immigration forms, additional fees may be collected pursuant to Section 8211. This fee limitation shall not apply to an attorney, who is also a notary public, who is rendering professional services regarding immigration matters.

(c) This section shall not be construed to exempt a notary public who enters data on an immigration form at the direction of a client, or otherwise performs the services of an immigration consultant, as defined by Section 22441 of the Business and Professions Code, from the requirements of Chapter 19.5 (commencing with Section 22440) of Division 8 of the Business and Professions Code. A notary public who is not qualified and bonded as an immigration consultant under Chapter 19.5 (commencing with Section 22440) of Division 8 of the Business and Professions Code may not enter data provided by a client on immigration forms nor otherwise perform the services of an immigration consultant.

§ 8224. Conflict of interest; financial or beneficial interest in transaction; exceptions

A notary public who has a direct financial or beneficial interest in a transaction shall not perform any notarial act in connection with such transaction.

For purposes of this section, a notary public has a direct financial or beneficial interest in a transaction if the notary public:

(a) With respect to a financial transaction, is named, individually, as a principal to the transaction.

(b) With respect to real property, is named, individually, as a grantor, grantee, mortgagor, mortgagee, trustor, trustee, beneficiary, vendor, vendee, lessor, or lessee, to the transaction.

For purposes of this section, a notary public has no direct financial or beneficial interest in a transaction where the notary public acts in the capacity of an agent, employee, insurer, attorney, escrow, or lender for a person having a direct financial or beneficial interest in the transaction.

§ 8224.1. Writings, depositions or affidavits of notary public; prohibitions against proof or taking by that notary public

A notary public shall not take the acknowledgment or proof of instruments of writing executed by the notary public nor shall depositions or affidavits of the notary public be taken by the notary public.

§ 8225. Improper notarial acts, solicitation, coercion or influence of performance; misdemeanor

(a) Any person who solicits, coerces, or in any manner influences a notary public to perform an improper notarial act knowing that act to be an improper notarial act, including any act required of a notary public under Section 8206, shall be guilty of a misdemeanor.

(b) Notwithstanding any other limitation of time described in Section 802 of the Penal Code, or any other provision of law, prosecution for a violation of this offense shall be commenced within four years after discovery of the commission of the offense, or within four years after the completion of the offense, whichever is later.

(c) The penalty provided by this section is not an exclusive remedy, and does not affect any other relief or remedy provided by law.

§ 8227.1. Unlawful acts by one not a notary public; misdemeanor

It shall be a misdemeanor for any person who is not a duly commissioned, qualified, and acting notary public for the State of California to do any of the following:

(a) Represent or hold himself or herself out to the public or to any person as being entitled to act as a notary public.

(b) Assume, use or advertise the title of notary public in such a manner as to convey the impression that the person is a notary public.

(c) Purport to act as a notary public.

§ 8227.3. Unlawful acts by one not a notary public; deeds of trust on single-family residences; felony

Any person who is not a duly commissioned, qualified, and acting notary public who does any of the acts prohibited by Section 8227.1 in relation to any document or instrument affecting title to, placing an encumbrance on, or placing an interest secured by a mortgage or deed of trust on, real property consisting of a single-family residence containing not more than four dwelling units, is guilty of a felony.

§ 8228. Enforcement of chapter; examination of notarial books, records, etc.

The Secretary of State or a peace officer, as defined in Sections 830.1, 830.2, and 830.3 of the Penal Code, possessing reasonable suspicion and acting in his or her official capacity and within his or her authority, may enforce the provisions of this chapter through the examination of a notary public's books, records, letters, contracts, and other pertinent documents relating to the official acts of the notary public.

§ 8228.1. Willful failure to perform duty or control notarial seal

(a) Any notary public who willfully fails to perform any duty required of a notary public under Section 8206, or who willfully fails to keep the seal of the notary public under the direct and exclusive control of the notary public, or who surrenders the seal of the notary public to any person not otherwise authorized by law to possess the seal of the notary, shall be guilty of a misdemeanor.

(b) Notwithstanding any other limitation of time described in Section 802 of the Penal Code or any other provision of law, prosecution for a violation of this offense shall be commenced within four years after discovery of the commission of the offense, or within four years after the completion of the offense, whichever is later.

(c) The penalty provided by this section is not an exclusive remedy, and does not affect any other relief or remedy provided by law.

§ 8230. Identification of affiant; verification

If a notary public executes a jurat and the statement sworn or subscribed to is contained in a document purporting to identify the affiant, and includes the birthdate or age of the person and a purported photograph or finger or thumbprint of the person so swearing or subscribing, the notary public shall require, as a condition to executing the jurat, that the person verify the birthdate or age contained in the statement by showing either:

(a) A certified copy of the person's birth certificate, or

(b) An identification card or driver's license issued by the Department of Motor Vehicles.

For the purposes of preparing for submission of forms required by the United States Immigration and Naturalization Service, and only for such purposes, a notary public may also accept for identification any documents or declarations acceptable to the United States Immigration and Naturalization Service.

* * *

§ 1360. Necessity of taking constitutional oath

Unless otherwise provided, following any election or appointment and before any officer enters on the duties of his or her office, he or she shall take and subscribe the oath or affirmation set forth in Section 3 of Article XX of the Constitution of California.

§ 1362. Administration by authorized officer

Unless otherwise provided, the oath may be taken before any officer authorized to administer oaths.

§ 6100. Performance of services; officers; notaries public

Officers of the state, or of a county or judicial district, shall not perform any official services unless upon the payment of the fees prescribed by law for the performance of the services, except as provided in this chapter.

This section shall not be construed to prohibit any notary public, except a notary public whose fees are required by law to be remitted to the state or any other public agency, from performing notarial services without charging a fee.

§ 6106. Pensions

Neither the State, nor any county or city, nor any public officer or body acting in his official capacity on behalf of the State, any county, or city, including notaries public, shall receive any fee or compensation for services rendered in an affidavit, or application relating to the securing of a pension, or the payment of a pension voucher, or any matter relating thereto.

§ 6107. Veterans

(a) A public entity, including the state, a county, city, or other political subdivision, or any officer or employee thereof, including notaries public, shall not demand or receive any fee or compensation for doing any of the following:

(1) Recording, indexing, or issuing certified copies of any discharge, certificate of service, certificate of satisfactory service, notice of separation, or report of separation of any member of the Armed Forces of the United States.

(2) Furnishing a certified copy of, or searching for, any public record that is to be used in an application or claim for a pension, allotment, allowance, compensation, insurance (including automatic insurance), or any other benefits under any act of Congress for service in the Armed Forces of the United States or under any law of this state relating to veterans' benefits.

(3) Furnishing a certified copy of, or searching for, any public record that is required by the Veterans Administration to be used in determining the eligibility of any person to participate in benefits made available by the Veterans Administration.

(4) Rendering any other service in connection with an application or claim referred to in paragraph (2) or (3).

(b) A certified copy of any record referred to in subdivision (a) may be made available only to one of the following:

(1) The person who is the subject of the record upon presentation of proper photo identification.

(2) A family member or legal representative of the person who is the subject of the record upon presentation of proper photo identification and certification of their relationship to the subject of the record.

(3) A state, county, or city office that provides veteran's benefits services upon written request of that office.

(4) A United States official upon written request of that official. A public officer or employee is liable on his or her official bond for failure or refusal to render the services.

§ 6108.   Oaths of office; claim against counties

No officer of a county or judicial district shall charge or receive any fee or compensation for administering or certifying the oath of office or for filing or swearing to any claim or demand against any county in the State.

§ 6109.   Receipt of fees; written account; officer liability

Every officer of a county or judicial district, upon receiving any fees for official duty or service, may be required by the person paying the fees to make out in writing and to deliver to the person a particular account of the fees. The account shall specify for what the fees, respectively, accrued, and the officer shall receipt it. If the officer refuses or neglects to do so when required, he is liable to the person paying the fees in treble the amount so paid.

§ 6110.   Performance of services following payment; officer liability

Upon payment of the fees required by law, the officer shall perform the services required. For every failure or refusal to do so, the officer is liable upon his official bond.

§ 6203.   False certificate or writing by officer

(a) Every officer authorized by law to make or give any certificate or other writing is guilty of a misdemeanor if he or she makes and delivers as true any certificate or writing containing statements which he or she knows to be false.

(b) Notwithstanding any other limitation of time described in Section 802 of the Penal Code, or any other provision of law, prosecution for a violation of this offense shall be commenced within four years after discovery of the commission of the offense, or within four years after the completion of the offense, whichever is later.

(c) The penalty provided by this section is not an exclusive remedy, and does not affect any other relief or remedy provided by law.

§ 6800.   Computation of time in which act is to be done

The time in which any act provided by law is to be done is computed by excluding the first day, and including the last, unless the last day is a holiday, and then it is also excluded.

§ 27287.   Acknowledgment of execution or proof by subscribing witness required before recording; exceptions

* * * before an instrument can be recorded its execution shall be acknowledged by the person executing it, or if executed by a corporation, by its president or secretary or other person executing it on behalf of the corporation, or, except for any power of attorney, quitclaim deed, grant deed, mortgage, deed of trust, security agreement, or other document affecting real property, proved by subscribing witness or as provided in Sections 1198 and 1199 of the Civil Code, and the acknowledgment or proof certified as prescribed by law. This section shall not apply to a trustee's deed resulting from a decree of foreclosure, or a nonjudicial foreclosure pursuant to Section 2924 of the Civil Code, or to a deed of reconveyance.

§ 66433.   Content and form; application of article

The content and form of final maps shall be governed by the provisions of this article.

§ 66436.   Statement of consent; necessity; exceptions; nonliability for omission of signature; notary acknowledgment

(a) A statement, signed and acknowledged by all parties having any record title interest in the subdivided real property, consenting to the preparation and recordation of the final map is required, * * *

(c) A notary acknowledgment shall be deemed complete for recording without the official seal of the notary, so long as the name of the notary, the county of the notary's principal place of business, and the notary's commission expiration date are typed or printed below or immediately adjacent to the notary's signature in the acknowledgment.

CIVIL CODE

§ 14.   Words and phrases; construction; tense; gender; number

* * * signature or subscription includes mark, when the person cannot write, his name being written near it, by a person who writes his own name as a witness; provided, that when a signature is by mark it must in order that the same may be acknowledged or may serve as the signature to any sworn statement be witnessed by two persons who must subscribe their own names as witnesses thereto. * * *

§ 1181.   Notaries public; officers before whom proof or acknowledgment may be made

The proof or acknowledgment of an instrument may be made before a notary public at any place within this state, or within the county or city and county in this state in which the officer specified below was elected or appointed, before either:

(a) A clerk of a superior court.

(b) A county clerk.

(c) A court commissioner.

(d) A retired judge of a municipal or justice court.

(e) A district attorney.

(f) A clerk of a board of supervisors.

(g) A city clerk.

(h) A county counsel.

(i) A city attorney.

(j) Secretary of the Senate.

(k) Chief Clerk of the Assembly.

§ 1185.   Acknowledgments; requisites

(a) The acknowledgment of an instrument shall not be taken unless the officer taking it has satisfactory evidence that the person making the acknowledgment is the individual who is described in and who executed the instrument.

(b) For the purposes of this section "satisfactory evidence" means the absence of information, evidence, or other circumstances that would lead a reasonable person to believe that the person making the acknowledgment is not the individual he or she claims to be and any one of the following:

(1)(A) The oath or affirmation of a credible witness personally known to the officer, whose identity is proven to the officer upon presentation of a document satisfying the requirements of paragraph (3) or (4), that the person making the acknowledgment is personally known to the witness and that each of the following are true:

(i) The person making the acknowledgment is the person named in the document.

(ii) The person making the acknowledgment is personally known to the witness.

(iii) That it is the reasonable belief of the witness that the circumstances of the person making the acknowledgment are such that it would be very difficult or impossible for that person to obtain another form of identification.

(iv) The person making the acknowledgment does not possess any of the identification documents named in paragraphs (3) and (4).

(v) The witness does not have a financial interest in the document being acknowledged and is not named in the document.

(B) A notary public who violates this section by failing to obtain the satisfactory evidence required by subparagraph (A) shall be subject to a civil penalty not exceeding ten thousand dollars ($10,000). An action to impose this civil penalty may be brought by the Secretary of State in an administrative proceeding or a public prosecutor in superior court, and shall be enforced as a civil judgment. A public prosecutor shall inform the secretary of any civil penalty imposed under this subparagraph.

(2) The oath or affirmation under penalty of perjury of two credible witnesses, whose identities are proven to the officer upon the presentation of a document satisfying the requirements of paragraph (3) or (4), that each statement in paragraph (1) is true.

(3) Reasonable reliance on the presentation to the officer of any one of the following, if the document is current or has been issued within five years:

(A) An identification card or driver's license issued by the Department of Motor Vehicles.

(B) A passport issued by the Department of State of the United States.

(C) An inmate identification card issued by the Department of Corrections and Rehabilitation, if the inmate is in custody in prison.

(D) Any form of inmate identification issued by a sheriff's department, if the inmate is in custody in a local detention facility.

(4) Reasonable reliance on the presentation of any one of the following, provided that a document specified in subparagraphs (A) to (F), inclusive, shall either be current or have been issued within five years and shall contain a photograph and description of the person named on it, shall be signed by the person, and shall bear a serial or other identifying number:

(A) A valid consular identification document issued by a consulate from the applicant's country of citizenship, or a valid passport from the applicant's country of citizenship.

(B) A driver's license issued by a state other than California or by a Canadian or Mexican public agency authorized to issue driver's licenses.

(C) An identification card issued by a state other than California.

(D) An identification card issued by any branch of the Armed Forces of the United States.

(E) An employee identification card issued by an agency or office of the State of California, or by an agency or office of a city, county, or city and county in this state.

(F) An identification card issued by a federally recognized tribal government.

(c) An officer who has taken an acknowledgment pursuant to this section shall be presumed to have operated in accordance with the provisions of law.

(d) A party who files an action for damages based on the failure of the officer to establish the proper identity of the person making the acknowledgment shall have the burden of proof in establishing the negligence or misconduct of the officer.

(e) A person convicted of perjury under this section shall forfeit any financial interest in the document.

§ 1188. Certificate of acknowledgment

An officer taking the acknowledgment of an instrument shall endorse thereon or attach thereto a certificate pursuant to Section 1189.

§ 1189. Certificate of acknowledgment; form; sufficiency of out of state acknowledgment; force and effect of acknowledgment under prior laws

(a)(1) Any certificate of acknowledgment taken within this state shall include a notice at the top of the certificate of acknowledgment in an enclosed box stating: "A notary public or other officer completing this certificate verifies only the identity of the individual who signed the document to which this certificate is attached, and not the truthfulness, accuracy, or validity of that document." This notice shall be legible.

(2) The physical format of the boxed notice at the top of the certificate of acknowledgment required pursuant to paragraph (3) is an example, for purposes of illustration and not limitation, of the physical format of a boxed notice fulfilling the requirements of paragraph (1).

(3) A certificate of acknowledgment taken within this state shall be in the following form:

> A notary public or other officer completing this
> certificate verifies only the identity of the
> individual who signed the document to which this
> certificate is attached, and not the truthfulness,
> accuracy, or validity of that document.

State of California ⎫
County of _____ ⎬
                    ⎭
   On _____ before me, (here insert name and title of the officer), personally appeared

_____

_____

_____

_____, who proved to me on
the basis of satisfactory evidence to be the person(s) whose name(s) is/are subscribed to the
within instrument and acknowledged to me that he/she/they executed the same in his/her/their
authorized capacity(ies), and that by his/her/their signature(s) on the instrument the person(s),
or the entity upon behalf of which the person(s) acted, executed the instrument.

I certify under PENALTY OF PERJURY under the laws of the State of California that the
foregoing paragraph is true and correct.

WITNESS my hand and official seal.

Signature _____   (Seal)

   (4) A notary public who willfully states as true any material fact that he or she knows to be
false shall be subject to a civil penalty not exceeding ten thousand dollars ($10,000). An action
to impose a civil penalty under this subdivision may be brought by the Secretary of State in an
administrative proceeding or any public prosecutor in superior court, and shall be enforced as
a civil judgment. A public prosecutor shall inform the secretary of any civil penalty imposed
under this section.

   (b) Any certificate of acknowledgment taken in another place shall be sufficient in this state
if it is taken in accordance with the laws of the place where the acknowledgment is made.

   (c) On documents to be filed in another state or jurisdiction of the United States, a California
notary public may complete any acknowledgment form as may be required in that other state
or jurisdiction on a document, provided the form does not require the notary to determine or
certify that the signer holds a particular representative capacity or to make other determinations
and certifications not allowed by California law.

   (d) An acknowledgment provided prior to January 1, 1993, and conforming to applicable
provisions of former Sections 1189, 1190, 1190a, 1190.1, 1191, and 1192, as repealed by
Chapter 335 of the Statutes of 1990, shall have the same force and effect as if those sections
had not been repealed.

§ 1190. Certificate of acknowledgment as prima facie evidence; duly authorized person

   The certificate of acknowledgment of an instrument executed on behalf of an incorporated or
unincorporated entity by a duly authorized person in the form specified in Section 1189 shall
be prima facie evidence that the instrument is the duly authorized act of the entity named in the
instrument and shall be conclusive evidence thereof in favor of any good faith purchaser, lessee,
or encumbrancer. "Duly authorized person," with respect to a domestic or foreign corporation,
includes the president, vice president, secretary, and assistant secretary of the corporation.

§ 1193. Certificate of acknowledgment; authentication

   Officers taking and certifying acknowledgments or proof of instruments for record, must
authenticate their certificates by affixing thereto their signatures, followed by the names
of their offices; also, their seals of office, if by the laws of the State or country where the
acknowledgment or proof is taken, or by authority of which they are acting, they are required
to have official seals.

§ 1195. Proof of execution; methods; certificate form

(a) Proof of the execution of an instrument, when not acknowledged, may be made by any of the following:

(1) By the party executing it, or either of them.

(2) By a subscribing witness.

(3) By other witnesses, in cases mentioned in Section 1198.

(b) (1) Proof of the execution of a power of attorney, grant deed, mortgage, deed of trust, quitclaim deed, security agreement, or any instrument affecting real property is not permitted pursuant to Section 27287 of the Government Code, though proof of the execution of a trustee's deed or deed of reconveyance is permitted.

(2) Proof of the execution for any instrument requiring a notary public to obtain a thumbprint from the party signing the document in the notary public's journal is not permitted.

(c) Any certificate for proof of execution taken within this state shall include a notice at the top of the certificate for proof of execution in an enclosed box stating: "A notary public or other officer completing this certificate verifies only the identity of the individual who signed the document to which this certificate is attached, and not the truthfulness, accuracy, or validity of that document." This notice shall be legible.

(d) The physical format of the boxed notice at the top of the certificate for proof of execution required pursuant to subdivision (e) is an example, for purposes of illustration and not limitation, of the physical format of a boxed notice fulfilling the requirements of subdivision (c).

(e) A certificate for proof of execution taken within this state shall be in the following form:

> A notary public or other officer completing this
> certificate verifies only the identity of the
> individual who signed the document to which this
> certificate is attached, and not the truthfulness,
> accuracy, or validity of that document.

State of California ⎫ ss.
County of _____ ⎭

On _____ (date), before me, _____ (name and title of officer), personally appeared _____ (name of subscribing witness), proved to me to be the person whose name is subscribed to the within instrument, as a witness thereto, on the oath of _____ (name of credible witness), a credible witness who is known to me and provided a satisfactory identifying document. _____ (name of subscribing witness), being by me duly sworn, said that he/she was present and saw/heard _____ (name[s] of principal[s]), the same person(s) described in and whose name(s) is/are subscribed to the within or attached instrument in his/her/their authorized capacity(ies) as (a) party (ies) thereto, execute or acknowledge executing the same, and that said affiant subscribed his/her name to the within or attached instrument as a witness at the request of _____ (name[s] of principal[s]).

WITNESS my hand and official seal.

Signature _____ (Seal)

§ 1196. Subscribing witness; establishment of identity

A witness shall be proved to be a subscribing witness by the oath of a credible witness who provides the officer with any document satisfying the requirements of paragraph (3) or (4) of subdivision (b) of Section 1185.

§ 1197. Subscribing witness; items to be proved

The subscribing witness must prove that the person whose name is subscribed to the instrument as a party is the person described in it, and that such person executed it, and that the witness subscribed his name thereto as a witness.

§ 1633.11.   Notarization and signature under penalty of perjury requirements

(a) If a law requires that a signature be notarized, the requirement is satisfied with respect to an electronic signature if an electronic record includes, in addition to the electronic signature to be notarized, the electronic signature of a notary public together with all other information required to be included in a notarization by other applicable law.

* * *

§ 1633.12.   Retaining records; electronic satisfaction

(a) If a law requires that a record be retained, the requirement is satisfied by retaining an electronic record of the information in the record, if the electronic record reflects accurately the information set forth in the record at the time it was first generated in its final form as an electronic record or otherwise, and the electronic record remains accessible for later reference.

(b) A requirement to retain a record in accordance with subdivision (a) does not apply to any information the sole purpose of which is to enable the record to be sent, communicated, or received.

(c) A person may satisfy subdivision (a) by using the services of another person if the requirements of subdivision (a) are satisfied.

(d) If a law requires a record to be retained in its original form, or provides consequences if the record is not retained in its original form, that law is satisfied by an electronic record retained in accordance with subdivision (a).

(e) If a law requires retention of a check, that requirement is satisfied by retention of an electronic record of the information on the front and back of the check in accordance with subdivision (a).

(f) A record retained as an electronic record in accordance with subdivision (a) satisfies a law requiring a person to retain a record for evidentiary, audit, or like purposes, unless a law enacted after the effective date of this title specifically prohibits the use of an electronic record for a specified purpose.

(g) This section does not preclude a governmental agency from specifying additional requirements for the retention of a record subject to the agency's jurisdiction.

CODE OF CIVIL PROCEDURE

§ 12a.   Computation of time; holidays; application of section

(a) If the last day for the performance of any act provided or required by law to be performed within a specified period of time is a holiday, then that period is hereby extended to and including the next day that is not a holiday. For purposes of this section, "holiday" means all day on Saturdays, all holidays specified in Section 135 and, to the extent provided in Section 12b, all days that by terms of Section 12b are required to be considered as holidays.

* * *

§ 1935.   Subscribing witness defined

A subscribing witness is one who sees a writing executed or hears it acknowledged, and at the request of the party thereupon signs his name as a witness.

§ 2093.   Officers authorized to administer oaths or affirmations

(a) A court, judge or clerk of a court, justice, notary public, and officer or person authorized to take testimony in an action or proceeding, or to decide upon evidence, has the power to administer oaths or affirmations.

(b) (1) A shorthand reporter certified pursuant to Article 3 (commencing with Section 8020) of Chapter 13 of Division 3 of the Business and Professions Code has the power to administer oaths and affirmations and may perform the duties of the deposition officer pursuant to Chapter 9 (commencing with Section 2025.010) of Title 4. The certified shorthand reporter is entitled to receive fees for services rendered during a deposition, including fees for deposition services, as specified in subdivision (c) of Section 8211 of the Government Code.

(2) This subdivision also applies to depositions taken by telephone or other remote electronic means as specified in Chapter 2 (commencing with Section 2017.010) and Chapter 9 (commencing with Section 2025.010) of Title 4.

(c)(1) A former judge or justice of a court of record in the state who retired or resigned from office may administer oaths and affirmations, if the former judge or justice requests and receives a certification from the Commission on Judicial Performance pursuant to paragraph (2).

(2) The Commission on Judicial Performance shall issue a certification enabling a former judge or justice to administer oaths and affirmations if the following conditions are satisfied:

(A) The former judge or justice was not removed from office; was not censured and barred from receiving an assignment, appointment, or reference of work from any California state court; did not retire or resign from office with an agreement with the commission that the former judge or justice would not receive an assignment, appointment or reference of work from any California state court; and, at the time of the former judge or justice's retirement, resignation, or request for certification, a formal disciplinary proceeding was not pending or was resolved on the merits in the judge or justice's favor after his or her retirement or resignation and before the request for certification.

(B) A medical certification provided to the commission by the former judge or justice pursuant to paragraph (3) establishes one of the following:

(i) The former judge or justice does not have a medical condition that would impair his or her ability to administer oaths or affirmations.

(ii) The former judge or justice has a medical condition that may impair his or her ability to administer oaths and affirmations, but the condition does not impair his or her ability at the present time.

(3) The Commission on Judicial Performance may require an applicant to obtain a medical certification in order to receive or renew a certification to administer oaths and affirmations if, at the time of resignation or retirement, there is evidence in a disability application file or in a disciplinary investigation file of possible cognitive impairment affecting the judge or justice, or if the former judge or justice previously received a two-year certification to administer oaths and affirmations from the commission. The commission shall supply the required forms to an applicant upon request.

(4) If an applicant's medical certification indicates that the applicant has a medical condition that may impair his or her ability to administer oaths and affirmations, but the condition does not impair his or her ability at the time the medical certification is submitted with the application, the Commission on Judicial Performance shall issue a certification to administer oaths and affirmations pursuant to paragraph (2), but the certification is only valid for a period of two years from the date of issuance.

(5) Notwithstanding paragraph (1), a former judge or justice of a court of record who received a certification to administer oaths and affirmations from the Commission on Judicial Performance prior to January 1, 2018, may continue to administer oaths and affirmations until the expiration of the certification, at which time he or she may reapply for certification pursuant to paragraph (2).

(6) The Commission on Judicial Performance may charge a regulatory fee not to exceed fifteen dollars ($15) for each certification application submitted pursuant to this subdivision to cover its costs, including costs to review a medical certification.

(d) A rule or regulation regarding the confidentiality of proceedings of the Commission on Judicial Performance does not prohibit the commission from issuing a certificate as provided for in this section.

(e)   The administration of an oath or affirmation pursuant to this section without pay does not violate Section 75060.6 of the Government Code.

* * *

§ 2094.   Oath to witness; form

(a) An oath, affirmation, or declaration in an action or a proceeding, may be administered by obtaining an affirmative response to one of the following questions:

(1) "Do you solemnly state that the evidence you shall give in this issue (or matter) shall be the truth, the whole truth, and nothing but the truth, so help you God?"

(2) "Do you solemnly state, under penalty of perjury, that the evidence that you shall give in this issue (or matter) shall be the truth, the whole truth, and nothing but the truth?"

* * *

ELECTIONS CODE

§ 8080.   Fee for verification

No fee or charge shall be made or collected by any officer for verifying any nomination document or circulator's affidavit.

COMMERCIAL CODE

§ 3505.   Protest; Noting for Protest

* * *

(b) A protest is a certificate of dishonor made by a United States consul or vice consul, or a notary public during the course and scope of employment with a financial institution or other person authorized to administer oaths by the laws of any other state, government, or country in the place where dishonor occurs. It may be made upon information satisfactory to that person. The protest shall identify the instrument and certify either that presentment has been made or, if not made, the reason why it was not made, and that the instrument has been dishonored by nonacceptance or nonpayment. The protest may also certify that notice of dishonor has been given to some or all parties.

PROBATE CODE

§ 4307.   Certified copies of power of attorney

(a) A copy of a power of attorney certified under this section has the same force and effect as the original power of attorney.

(b) A copy of a power of attorney may be certified by any of the following:

(1) An attorney authorized to practice law in this state.

(2) A notary public in this state.

(3) An official of a state or of a political subdivision who is authorized to make certifications.

(c) The certification shall state that the certifying person has examined the original power of attorney and the copy and that the copy is a true and correct copy of the original power of attorney.

(d) Nothing in this section is intended to create an implication that a third person may be liable for acting in good faith reliance on a copy of a power of attorney that has not been certified under this section.

PENAL CODE

§ 17. Felony; misdemeanor; infraction; classification of offenses

(a) A felony is a crime that is punishable with death, by imprisonment in the state prison, or notwithstanding any other provision of law, by imprisonment in a county jail under the provisions of subdivision (h) of Section 1170. Every other crime or public offense is a misdemeanor except those offenses that are classified as infractions. * * *

§ 115.5. Filing false or forged documents relating to single-family residences; punishment; false statement to notary public

(a) Every person who files any false or forged document or instrument with the county recorder which affects title to, places an encumbrance on, or places an interest secured by a mortgage or deed of trust on, real property consisting of a single-family residence containing not more than four dwelling units, with knowledge that the document is false or forged, is punishable, in addition to any other punishment, by a fine not exceeding seventy-five thousand dollars ($75,000).

(b) Every person who makes a false sworn statement to a notary public, with knowledge that the statement is false, to induce the notary public to perform an improper notarial act on an instrument or document affecting title to, or placing an encumbrance on, real property consisting of a single-family residence containing not more than four dwelling units is guilty of a felony.

§ 118. Perjury defined; evidence necessary to support conviction

(a) Every person who, having taken an oath that he or she will testify, declare, depose, or certify truly before any competent tribunal, officer, or person, in any of the cases in which the oath may by law of the State of California be administered, willfully and contrary to the oath, states as true any material matter which he or she knows to be false, and every person who testifies, declares, deposes, or certifies under penalty of perjury in any of the cases in which the testimony, declarations, depositions, or certification is permitted by law of the State of California under penalty of perjury and willfully states as true any material matter which he or she knows to be false, is guilty of perjury.

This subdivision is applicable whether the statement, or the testimony, declaration, deposition, or certification is made or subscribed within or without the State of California.

(b) No person shall be convicted of perjury where proof of falsity rests solely upon contradiction by testimony of a single person other than the defendant. Proof of falsity may be established by direct or indirect evidence.

§ 126. Punishment

Perjury is punishable by imprisonment pursuant to subdivision (h) of Section 1170 for two, three or four years.

§ 470. Forgery; signatures or seals; corruption of records

* * *

(b) Every person who, with the intent to defraud, counterfeits or forges the seal or handwriting of another is guilty of forgery.

* * *

(d) Every person who, with the intent to defraud, falsely makes, alters, forges, or counterfeits, utters, publishes, passes or attempts or offers to pass, as true and genuine, any of the following items, knowing the same to be false, altered, forged, or counterfeited, is guilty of forgery: ... or falsifies the acknowledgment of any notary public, or any notary public who issues an acknowledgment knowing it to be false; or any matter described in subdivision (b).

* * *

§ 473. Forgery; punishment

Forgery is punishable by imprisonment in a county jail for not more than one year, or by imprisonment pursuant to subdivision (h) of Section 1170.

§ 830.3. Peace officers; employing agencies; authority

The following persons are peace officers whose authority extends to any place in the state for the purpose of performing their primary duty or when making an arrest pursuant to Section 836 as to any public offense with respect to which there is immediate danger to person or property, or of the escape of the perpetrator of that offense, or pursuant to Section 8597 or 8598 of the Government Code. * * *

(o) Investigators of the office of the Secretary of State designated by the Secretary of State, provided that the primary duty of these peace officers shall be the enforcement of the law as prescribed in Chapter 3 (commencing with Section 8200) of Division 1 of Title 2 of, and Section 12172.5 of, the Government Code. * * *

BUSINESS AND PROFESSIONS CODE

§ 22449. Deferred Action for Childhood Arrivals program; price gouging; penalties

(a) Immigration consultants, attorneys, notaries public, and organizations accredited by the United States Board of Immigration Appeals shall be the only individuals authorized to charge clients or prospective clients fees for providing consultations, legal advice, or notary public services, respectively, associated with filing an application under the federal Deferred Action for Childhood Arrivals program announced by the United States Secretary of Homeland Security on June 15, 2012.

(b)(1) Immigration consultants, attorneys, notaries public, and organizations accredited by the United States Board of Immigration Appeals shall be prohibited from participating in practices that amount to price gouging when a client or prospective client solicits services associated with filing an application for deferred action for childhood arrivals as described in subdivision (a).

(2) For the purposes of this section, "price gouging" means any practice that has the effect of pressuring the client or prospective client to purchase services immediately because purchasing them at a later time will result in the client or prospective client paying a higher price for the same services.

(c)(1) In addition to the civil and criminal penalties described in Section 22445, a violation of this section by an attorney shall be cause for discipline by the State Bar pursuant to Chapter 4 (commencing with Section 6000) of Division 3.

(2) In addition to the civil and criminal penalties described in Section 22445, a violation of this section by a notary public shall be cause for the revocation or suspension of his or her commission as a notary public by the Secretary of State and the application of any other applicable penalties pursuant to Chapter 3 (commencing with Section 8200) of Division 1 of Title 2 of the Government Code.

INDEX

CPSIA information can be obtained
at www.ICGtesting.com
Printed in the USA
LVHW051500040619
620111LV00003B/543/P

9 780359 572038